Sushi Mastery:

100 Recipes from Nakamoto's Kitchen

By Takeshi Nakamoto

Copyright © 2024 Takeshi Nakamoto

All Rights Reserved

Disclaimer

Reasonable care has been taken to ensure that the information presented in this book is accurate. However, the reader should understand that the information provided does not constitute legal, medical or professional advice of any kind.

No Liability: this product is supplied "as is" and without warranties. All warranties, express or implied, are hereby disclaimed. Use of this product constitutes acceptance of the "No Liability" policy. If you do not agree with this policy, you are not permitted to use or distribute this product.

We shall not be liable for any losses or damages whatsoever

(including, without limitation, consequential loss or damage) directly or indirectly arising from the use of this product.

SUSHI MASTERY: 100 RECIPES FROM NAKAMOTO'S KITCHEN

Table of Contents:

Introduction:

Welcome to a world where culinary art meets the delicate dance of tradition and innovation. I am Takeshi Nakamoto, and I invite you to embark on a vibrant journey through the art of sushi-making—a craft that transforms humble ingredients into masterpieces of flavor and elegance. Sushi is not just food; it is a celebration of life, a symphony of textures and tastes that tell a story with every bite. In this book, "Sushi Mastery: 100 Recipes from Nakamoto's Kitchen," we will explore the depths of this iconic Japanese dish, giving you the tools to create sushi that is both authentic and uniquely your own.

In these pages, you will find a collection of 100 carefully curated recipes, each designed to guide you through the fascinating world of sushi. Whether you are a novice eager to learn the basics or a seasoned chef looking to expand your repertoire, this cookbook offers something for everyone. From the foundations of perfect sushi rice and the artful slicing of sashimi to the creative flair of specialty rolls and the elegance of seasonal sushi, each recipe is a steppingstone on your path to sushi mastery.

What makes the recipes in this book unique is the fusion of time-honored techniques with modern innovations. Sushi is an art form rooted in precision and tradition, but it is also a canvas for creativity. In my kitchen, I have always sought to honor the past while embracing the future, blending traditional flavors with unexpected twists to create dishes that surprise and delight. You will learn how to prepare classics like the Classic Maguro Nigiri and Dragon Roll, but also experience the thrill of discovering new creations like the Firecracker Roll or the decadent Truffle Tuna Tartar.

The journey begins with the essentials: the perfect sushi rice, the crisp nori, and the vibrant wasabi. These may seem like simple ingredients, but they are the foundation upon which all great sushi is built. As you master these basics, you will find yourself more confident in experimenting with advanced techniques and flavors, such as crafting the intricate Volcano Roll or the luxurious Lobster Tempura Roll.

As we delve into the realm of sashimi, you will learn to appreciate the subtle beauty of silken slices of Salmon Sashimi or the sweet ocean freshness of Scallop Sashimi. These dishes celebrate the purity of each ingredient, allowing their natural flavors to shine through with minimal intervention.

In the world of maki and nigiri, we explore the harmony of ingredients, where each element plays its part in creating a balanced and delightful experience. From the fiery Spicy Tuna Roll to the creamy perfection of the Salmon Avocado Roll, each recipe is an opportunity to express your culinary vision.

But this journey is not just about fish. Our exploration extends to vegetarian sushi, where the freshness of garden ingredients takes center stage. Imagine the nutty delight of Spinach Gomae Maki or the comforting layers of a Sweet Potato Roll.

And dare I mention dessert sushi? Here, the unexpected becomes the norm, as we indulge in Sweet Mochi Sushi or the exotic flavor of Mango Sticky Rice Sushi. These sweet creations challenge the traditional boundaries of sushi, inviting you to reimagine what sushi can be.

This cookbook is divided into categories that guide you along this journey: Sushi Rice and Essentials, Sashimi Selections, Nigiri Creations, Maki Rolls, Specialty Rolls, Vegetarian Sushi, Advanced Sushi Techniques, Dessert Sushi, Innovative Sushi, and Festive and Seasonal Sushi. Each section is a chapter in your culinary adventure, filled with step-by-step guidance and insights to help you perfect your skills.

So, dear reader, tie on your apron, sharpen your knives, and prepare to immerse yourself in a culinary experience that transcends borders and traditions. Let us embrace the spirit of innovation while honoring the soul of sushi. Welcome to "Sushi Mastery: 100 Recipes from Nakamoto's Kitchen," where your journey to becoming a sushi master begins.

Sushi Rice and Essentials

1. Perfect Sushi Rice: The Foundation of Flavor

Ah, the humble grain of rice! It's the canvas upon which sushi's masterpiece is painted. Mastering the perfect sushi rice is like tuning an instrument—once you get it right, everything sings in harmony!

Preparation time: 10 minutes
Cooking time: 20 minutes
Ready-in time: 1 hour
Serving size: 4 people

Ingredients:
2 cups sushi rice
2 cups water
1/3 cup rice vinegar
3 tablespoons sugar
1 teaspoon salt

Instructions:

First, let's give our rice the spa treatment it deserves. Rinse 2 cups of sushi rice under cold water, gently swirling it around with your fingers. Do this until the water runs clear—it's like washing away the day's stress.

Next, let the rice soak in water for about 30 minutes. This resting period is crucial, like a samurai meditating before battle. After soaking, drain the rice.

Place the drained rice in a rice cooker and add 2 cups of water. Switch on the rice cooker and let it do its magic. If you don't have a rice cooker, use a pot with a tight-fitting lid. Bring the rice to a boil, then reduce the heat to low, cover it, and let it simmer for 20 minutes. Once done, let it rest for another 10 minutes without lifting the lid. Patience, my friend, patience!

While the rice cooks, let's prepare the seasoning. In a small saucepan over low heat, combine 1/3 cup rice vinegar, 3 tablespoons sugar, and 1 teaspoon salt. Stir until the sugar and salt dissolve completely. Do not let it boil. Remove from the heat and let it cool.

Now, transfer your cooked rice to a large wooden or plastic bowl. Pour the seasoned vinegar mixture over the rice. Using a wooden spatula, gently fold the rice, cutting through it with a slicing motion. This ensures that each grain is evenly coated without becoming mushy. Remember to fan the rice with a hand fan or a piece of cardboard while mixing. This cools the rice quickly and gives it a glossy finish.

Once the rice has cooled to room temperature, it's ready to be the star of your sushi creations!

Ah, the journey of a thousand miles begins with a single grain of rice. You've taken the first step towards sushi mastery. Now, go forth and create delicious memories, one sushi roll at a time!

2. Classic Vinegar Blend: Elevate Your Rice

Embrace the essence of traditional sushi-making with this vinegar blend that breathes life into each grain of rice. The secret lies in balancing the flavors to create a symphony that dances on your palate.

Preparation time: 10 minutes
Cooking time: 0 minutes
Ready-in time: 10 minutes
Serving size: 4 people

Ingredients:
1 cup rice vinegar
3 tablespoons sugar
2 teaspoons salt
2 tablespoons mirin

Instructions:

Alright, let's get started! First, grab a small saucepan and pour in the rice vinegar. Now, add the sugar and salt to the vinegar. You might be thinking, Trust me, it's just right. The sugar balances the sharpness of the vinegar while the salt enhances the overall flavor.

Next, place the saucepan over medium heat. You don't need to boil it; just gently heat until the sugar and salt are completely dissolved. Keep stirring constantly with a wooden spoon. This is a delicate process, almost like a tea ceremony – calm and deliberate.

Once everything is dissolved, add the mirin. This sweet rice wine adds a subtle depth to our blend. Give it a good stir and then remove the saucepan from the heat.

Let it cool down to room temperature. You can transfer it to a small bowl or a bottle for easy pouring. Your classic vinegar blend is ready to elevate your sushi rice to the next level.

Remember, the key is to mix the vinegar blend into the rice while it's still warm. Use a slicing motion with a rice paddle, almost like folding a delicate whipped cream. This ensures each grain is perfectly coated without being squashed.

And there you go! A timeless vinegar blend that transforms ordinary rice into the heart and soul of sushi.

"Bravo! You've just unlocked a cornerstone of sushi mastery. Every grain of rice thanks you for the love and care. Now, go forth and craft your sushi dreams with confidence and flair!"

Isn't that too much?

3. Nori Preparation: Crisp and Ready

Ah, the magic of nori! Elevate your sushi game with this essential step that ensures every bite is a crisp, umami-packed delight. Ready to turn that simple sheet of seaweed into a star performer?

Preparation time: 5 minutes
Cooking time: 5 minutes
Ready-in time: 10 minutes
Serving size: 4 people

Ingredients:
5 sheets of nori (seaweed)
1 teaspoon sesame oil
1 teaspoon sea salt

Instructions:

First, let's coax that nori into a state of crispy perfection. Lay your nori sheets flat on a clean, dry surface. Next, with a basting brush or a piece of paper towel, gently paint a whisper-thin layer of sesame oil across one side of each nori sheet. This is where the nori starts to get its personality!

Now, sprinkle a pinch of sea salt evenly over the oiled side. Not too much, just enough to add a subtle hint of that oceanic saltiness we crave in our sushi.

Heat a dry skillet over medium-high heat. You want it hot, but not smoking. Gently lay each nori sheet, oil-side up, on the hot skillet. Toast the nori for about 15-20 seconds on each side, until it turns crisp and slightly greenish. The aroma will tell you it's ready—listen to it!

Remove the toasted nori from the skillet and let it cool on a wire rack. This helps it stay crispy. If you find any parts that aren't as crisp as you'd like, just give them another quick toast in the skillet.

And there you have it! Your nori is now crisp, aromatic, and perfectly seasoned. Ready to wrap around sushi rice or any other delightful fillings you have in mind.

Remember, just as the ocean waves shape the shore, every detail shapes your sushi experience. Enjoy the crisp perfection and let each bite take you on a journey.

4. Fresh Wasabi: Grating the Green Gold

In the heart of Japan, nestled among misty mountains, grows a treasure unlike any other: fresh wasabi. This is not your average condiment – it's a delicacy that demands reverence. Today, we'll uncover the art of grating this green gold to elevate your sushi experience to celestial heights.

Preparation time: 5 minutes
Cooking time: 0 minutes
Ready-in time: 5 minutes
Serving size: 4 people

Ingredients:
1 fresh wasabi rhizome
A sharkskin or ceramic grater
A small dish

Instructions:

First, let's prepare our wasabi rhizome. Gently rinse it under cold water to remove any dirt. You want this jewel to be pristine. Now, with a vegetable peeler, carefully peel away the outer skin, revealing the vibrant green flesh beneath.

Holding the wasabi rhizome at a slight angle, begin to grate it using a sharkskin or ceramic grater. Yes, that's right, a sharkskin grater – it's traditional and gives the best texture. If you don't have one, a fine ceramic grater will do the trick. Grate in a circular motion, applying just enough pressure to break down the fibers and release the wasabi's full flavor.

As you grate, you'll notice the wasabi forming a soft, aromatic paste. Don't rush this process; savor it. The fresher the wasabi, the more intense and complex its flavor profile. Once you have a generous amount of paste, let it rest for a minute or two. This brief period allows the flavors to develop fully.

When you're ready, transfer the wasabi paste to a small dish. Serve immediately with your sushi, sashimi, or any dish that deserves this exquisite touch. Remember, fresh wasabi is best enjoyed right after grating, capturing its fiery kick and delicate sweetness at their peak.

Now, wasn't that a journey worth embarking on? Fresh wasabi is more than a condiment; it's an expression of nature's artistry. As you relish each bite, let the flavors transport you to those misty Japanese mountains. Until next time, keep exploring the wonders of sushi mastery!

5. Dashi Stock: The Umami Secret

Ah, Dashi! The heartbeat of Japanese cuisine, a simple broth yet profoundly transformative. Imagine the delicate dance of flavors, the ocean's whisper, the forest's murmur. This, my friends, is where our journey to umami begins.

Preparation time: 5 minutes
Cooking time: 15 minutes
Ready-in time: 20 minutes
Serving size: 4 people

Ingredients:
1 piece of kombu (about 4 inches)
4 cups of water
1 cup of bonito flakes

Instructions:

Alright, sushi aficionados, let's dive into the essence of umami. First, take a piece of kombu, about 4 inches, and gently wipe it with a damp cloth. No need for a thorough cleaning; we want to keep that marine essence intact.

Now, fill a pot with 4 cups of water and introduce the kombu to its new home. Let it soak for about 10 minutes to awaken its flavors. After this brief soak, turn the heat to medium and slowly bring the water to a near-simmer. Patience, my friends, is key here. Do not let it boil! We want to tease out the umami, not overwhelm it.

When you see tiny bubbles forming around the edges, it's time to remove the kombu. Thank it for its service and set it aside. Now, the magic continues. Add 1 cup of bonito flakes to the pot. Watch them dance and swirl, infusing the broth with their rich, smoky essence.

Let the bonito flakes steep for just a few minutes until they sink to the bottom, signaling they've bestowed all their goodness. Now, strain the liquid through a fine-mesh sieve or a cheesecloth-lined strainer into a clean bowl. And there you have it, the golden elixir of Japanese cuisine – your very own dashi stock.

This humble broth will elevate your dishes to new heights. Keep it close, treasure it, and let it be the secret to your culinary mastery. Now, go forth and create magic in your kitchen, my fellow sushi artisans!

6. Pickled Ginger Bliss: Sweet and Sharp

Ah, pickled ginger. A symphony of sweet and sharp, this beautiful condiment dances on your palate, cleansing and invigorating with each bite. It's not just a sidekick to sushi; it's a star in its own right. Let's embark on this flavorful journey together!

Preparation time: 15 minutes
Cooking time: 5 minutes
Ready-in time: 2 hours 20 minutes
Serving size: 4 people

Ingredients:
200 grams fresh young ginger
1 cup rice vinegar
1/2 cup granulated sugar
2 teaspoons sea salt
1 cup water
1 small beet (optional, for color)

Instructions:

First, let's bring the ginger to life. Take your fresh young ginger and peel it gently with a spoon. We want to keep it delicate. Slice the ginger as thinly as possible; a mandoline slicer can be your best friend here. Once sliced, sprinkle salt over the ginger and let it sit for about 5 minutes – this helps to soften and bring out the flavor. Rinse the ginger under cold water and pat it dry with a clean kitchen towel.

Now, we move to the stove. In a small saucepan, combine rice vinegar, sugar, and water. If you desire that beautiful pink hue often seen in pickled ginger, add a small piece of beet. Bring this mixture to a gentle boil, stirring until the sugar is completely dissolved. Once it's ready, remove the beet.

Place your ginger slices into a clean jar. Pour the hot vinegar mixture over the ginger, ensuring all slices are submerged. Let it cool to room temperature before sealing the jar with a lid.

Patience is key here. Allow the ginger to marinate in the fridge for at least 2 hours. Though, if you can wait overnight, the flavors will meld even more beautifully.

When ready, serve this pickled ginger alongside your sushi creations or enjoy it as a refreshing palate cleanser.

Ah, the taste of pickled ginger – a bite of pure bliss! I hope you enjoy making and savoring this delightful condiment. Remember, great sushi is all about balance, and this ginger is the perfect harmony. Until next time, happy cooking and joyful eating!

7. Tamagoyaki: The Sweet Egg Roll

In the heart of any sushi chef's repertoire lies the humble yet profoundly delightful tamagoyaki. It's a dish that dances between sweet and savory, bringing a smile with each bite. Let's embark on this flavorful journey together and make magic happen in your kitchen!

Preparation time: 10 minutes
Cooking time: 10 minutes
Ready-in time: 20 minutes
Serving size: 4 people

Ingredients:
6 large eggs
1 1/2 tablespoons sugar
1 1/2 tablespoons mirin (sweet rice wine)
1/2 teaspoon soy sauce
1/4 teaspoon salt
1 tablespoon vegetable oil

Instructions:

Alright, my friends, let's get started! First, crack those six large eggs into a bowl and whisk them until they blend into a smooth, golden liquid. Add in the sugar, mirin, soy sauce, and salt, and whisk again until everything is well combined. This mixture should be silky and slightly frothy.

Now, heat a rectangular tamagoyaki pan over medium heat. If you don't have a rectangular pan, a small round non-stick skillet will work just fine. Add a little vegetable oil to the pan, spreading it evenly with a paper towel.

Pour a thin layer of your egg mixture into the pan, just enough to cover the bottom. As soon as the edges start to set but the top is still a bit runny, use chopsticks or a spatula to gently roll the egg from one side to the other, like rolling up a scroll. Move the rolled egg to one side of the pan.

Add a bit more oil if needed, then pour another thin layer of the egg mixture into the empty part of the pan. Lift the rolled egg so the new layer can flow underneath it. Once this layer begins to set, roll the first roll back over it, creating a thicker roll. Repeat this process, adding more egg mixture and rolling until you've used up all the egg.

Once you have a nice, plump egg roll, let it cook for another minute to ensure it's fully set. Transfer the tamagoyaki to a bamboo sushi mat or a cutting board, letting it rest for a moment. Slice it into even pieces, about half an inch thick, and serve warm or at room temperature.

Ah, there you have it! A sweet and savory masterpiece that reflects the soul of Japanese culinary artistry. Enjoy every bite, and remember, the heart of cooking is joy. Until next time, keep your knives sharp and your spirits high!

8. Sushi Rice Balls: Onigiri Simplicity

In the heart of simplicity lies the essence of culinary perfection. Onigiri, the humble rice ball, carries with it the spirit of Japan – a delightful snack that's as comforting as it is versatile.

Preparation time: 20 minutes
Cooking time: 20 minutes
Ready-in time: 40 minutes
Serving size: 4 people

Ingredients:
2 cups sushi rice, cooked and cooled
1/2 teaspoon salt
4 sheets nori (seaweed), cut into strips
1/2 cup pickled plum (umeboshi), flaked
1/2 cup salted salmon, flaked
1/2 cup tuna with mayonnaise
1/2 cup pickled vegetables, finely chopped
Water for wetting hands

Instructions:

First, let's start by preparing our hands – yes, our hands! Wet them with a little water and then sprinkle on some salt. This not only helps in shaping the rice but also adds a subtle flavor to our onigiri.

Take a small handful of sushi rice, about the size of a tennis ball, and flatten it slightly in your palm. Now, it's time to choose your filling. Whether you favor the tangy punch of umeboshi, the savory delight of salted salmon, the creamy allure of tuna with mayo, or the crunch of pickled vegetables, place about a teaspoon of your chosen filling in the center of the rice.

Gently fold the rice around the filling, shaping it into a triangle or a round ball. Don't worry if it's not perfect; each onigiri carries its own charm. Press firmly but gently to ensure the filling is completely encased in rice.

Now, let's dress our onigiri. Wrap a strip of nori around the rice ball, letting the seaweed's natural stickiness secure it in place. The crispy texture of the nori contrasts beautifully with the soft rice.

Repeat these steps until all the rice and fillings are used. Arrange your onigiri on a plate, and they are ready to serve!

Embrace the simplicity, and you'll find the soul of Japanese cuisine in each bite. These delightful treats are perfect for any occasion – whether you're on the go or enjoying a quiet moment at home. Happy eating, and may your culinary journey be as vibrant as your imagination!

9. Ponzu Sauce: Citrus Infusion

Imagine the essence of citrus dancing with the depth of soy sauce, creating a symphony of flavors that whisper the secrets of umami to your taste buds. That's the magic of Ponzu Sauce, a versatile condiment that can elevate your sushi experience to celestial heights.

Preparation time: 10 minutes
Cooking time: 5 minutes
Ready-in time: 15 minutes
Serving size: 4 people

Ingredients:
1/2 cup soy sauce
1/4 cup lemon juice
1/4 cup lime juice
1/4 cup orange juice
2 tablespoons rice vinegar
1 tablespoon mirin
1 tablespoon bonito flakes
1 small piece kombu (dried kelp)
1 tablespoon freshly grated ginger

Instructions:

Gather your ingredients and let's embark on this flavorful journey. Start by mixing the soy sauce, lemon juice, lime juice, and orange juice in a medium bowl. Feel the vibrant citrus aromas wafting through the air.

Next, add the rice vinegar and mirin to the mixture. These elements introduce a touch of mellow sweetness and acidity that beautifully balances the tanginess of the citrus.

Now, let's invite the umami guests to the party. Toss in the bonito flakes and the small piece of kombu. These ingredients are like wise elders imparting depth and wisdom to our Ponzu Sauce.

Grate the fresh ginger and add it to the mix. Ginger adds a zing that will make your taste buds stand at attention, eager for the next bite.

Transfer the mixture to a small saucepan and gently heat it over low flame. Stir occasionally and let the ingredients mingle for about 5 minutes, but don't let it boil. We want a gentle infusion, not a harsh reduction.

Once done, remove the saucepan from heat and allow the mixture to cool. Strain the sauce into a clean jar, discarding the solids. Your Ponzu Sauce is now ready to grace your sushi, sashimi, or even grilled meats with its delightful, multifaceted character.

Ah, the joys of crafting a perfect Ponzu Sauce! It's like capturing a piece of culinary poetry in a bottle. Remember, this sauce is a canvas—don't be afraid to experiment and make it your own. Until next time, may your kitchen adventures be ever flavorful and fun!

10. Soy Sauce Reduction: Intensified Savory

In the heart of the kitchen, magic happens when the simplest ingredients merge to create a symphony of flavors. This soy sauce reduction will elevate your sushi creations to an art form, adding a deep, umami richness that's simply unforgettable.

Preparation time: 5 minutes
Cooking time: 20 minutes
Ready-in time: 25 minutes
Serving size: 4 people

Ingredients:
1 cup soy sauce
1/2 cup mirin
1/4 cup sake
2 tablespoons sugar
1 piece kombu (2 inches)
1 clove garlic, smashed
1 slice ginger (1 inch)

Instructions:

Alright, let's dance with these ingredients! Start by grabbing a small saucepan. Pour in the soy sauce, mirin, and sake. Feel the anticipation build as you add the sugar, giving it a gentle stir to dissolve. Now, let's invite the kombu into the mix, along with the garlic and ginger – these two will add a beautiful depth to our reduction.

Place the saucepan over medium heat and bring the mixture to a gentle simmer. You'll want to keep a watchful eye on it, stirring occasionally. As the sauce bubbles away, it will start to thicken, and the flavors will intensify. This is the magic happening right before your eyes!

After about 15 minutes, the sauce should have reduced by half. At this point, remove the kombu, garlic, and ginger. They've done their job, imparting their essence into our savory concoction. Allow the sauce to simmer for another 5 minutes, until it reaches a syrupy consistency.

Once you're satisfied with the thickness, remove the saucepan from the heat. Let the reduction cool slightly before transferring it to a serving bowl or a small pitcher. This luscious sauce is now ready to be drizzled over your sushi, adding that extra layer of umami that will have everyone coming back for more.

Ah, the joy of creating something so simple yet so profound! This soy sauce reduction is like a secret handshake between you and your taste buds. Until next time, keep your knives sharp and your flavors bold!

11. Salmon Sashimi: Silken Slices

Imagine the sea whispering secrets to you as you delicately slice through the tender flesh of a perfectly fresh salmon. This dish is simplicity itself, yet it speaks volumes of elegance and tradition, a true homage to the artistry of sushi.

Preparation time: 15 minutes
Cooking time: 0 minutes
Ready-in time: 15 minutes
Serving size: 4 people

Ingredients:
250 grams of fresh, high-quality salmon fillet
2 tablespoons soy sauce
1 tablespoon freshly squeezed lemon juice
1 teaspoon wasabi
1 small bunch of shiso leaves or fresh mint
Pickled ginger, for serving
Daikon radish, finely shredded, for garnish

Instructions:

First, let's prepare our stage. Ensure your salmon fillet is as fresh as the morning dew – it should smell like the ocean breeze, not like fish. Place the fillet in the freezer for about 15 minutes to firm it up; this makes slicing easier and more precise.

While the salmon chills, let's prepare the accompaniments. Mix the soy sauce and freshly squeezed lemon juice in a small bowl. This creates a tangy, savory dip that complements the richness of the salmon. Set aside.

Now, the star of our show returns. Using a very sharp knife, slice the salmon against the grain into thin, even slices – about a quarter-inch thick. Each slice should be a silken ribbon, almost translucent, and absolutely inviting.

Arrange the salmon slices artfully on a chilled platter. This isn't just food; it's an expression. Surround the salmon with a few shiso leaves or fresh mint for a burst of color and aromatic intrigue.

Place a small mound of freshly shredded daikon radish in the center of the platter. This adds a crunchy contrast and a visual flair. Position a few slices of pickled ginger around the edges – they are the zesty punctuation marks to our edible poetry.

Serve the salmon sashimi with the soy-lemon dip on the side, and a dab of wasabi for those who dare to dance with heat. Encourage your guests to dip a slice of salmon into the soy-lemon mixture, add a touch of wasabi, and savor the symphony of flavors.

Congratulations, you have just created a masterpiece worthy of applause! Each bite of this salmon sashimi is a journey to the heart of Japanese culinary tradition – elegant, pure, and unforgettable. Until our next culinary adventure, may your knives stay sharp and your fish always fresh!

12. Tuna Tataki: Seared Perfection

Picture this: a delicate dance of flavors and textures, where the tender tuna meets a sizzling hot pan for just the briefest of moments. This dish is a testament to the beauty of simplicity and precision. Let's embark on this culinary journey together, shall we?

Preparation time: 10 minutes
Cooking time: 5 minutes
Ready-in time: 15 minutes
Serving size: 4 people

Ingredients:
400g sashimi-grade tuna loin
1 tablespoon sesame oil
2 tablespoons soy sauce
1 tablespoon mirin
1 tablespoon rice vinegar
1 teaspoon grated ginger
1 clove garlic, minced
1 tablespoon sesame seeds (white or black)
1 small bunch of scallions, finely chopped
1 tablespoon vegetable oil
Sea salt and freshly ground black pepper, to taste

Instructions:

First things first, let's prep our beautiful tuna. Pat it dry with a paper towel and season it ever so lightly with a sprinkle of sea salt and freshly ground black pepper. This step sets the stage for our searing magic.

Now, in a small bowl, whisk together soy sauce, mirin, rice vinegar, grated ginger, and minced garlic. This will be our savory marinade. Place the tuna in the marinade for about 5 minutes, just enough time for it to soak up those incredible flavors without overpowering its natural essence.

While the tuna is marinating, heat the vegetable oil in a skillet over medium-high heat. We want it hot, but not smoking. Lay the tuna in the skillet and sear each side for about 30-45 seconds. Remember, we're aiming for a beautifully rare center with a nicely seared exterior. This is the essence of tataki, my friends!

Once seared to perfection, remove the tuna from the heat and let it rest for a moment. In the meantime, lightly toast the sesame seeds in another dry skillet until they're fragrant and golden.

Slice the tuna into thin, delicate pieces and arrange them on a serving platter. Drizzle with a bit of the remaining marinade, sprinkle with those toasted sesame seeds, and garnish with a generous pinch of finely chopped scallions. Voila! Tuna Tataki in all its glory.

Ah, there it is - a dish that sings with simplicity and elegance. Savor each bite, and let the flavors transport you to the shores of Japan. Until our next culinary adventure, remember: great sushi starts with respect for the ingredients and a passion for perfection. Enjoy!

13. Yellowtail Crudo: Citrus Marinated Delight

In the bustling heart of Tokyo, where tradition meets innovation, I discovered a simple yet profound truth: the freshest fish needs only a whisper of flavor to shine. This crudo embodies that philosophy, celebrating yellowtail's natural elegance with a bright citrus kiss.

Preparation time: 15 minutes
Cooking time: None
Ready-in time: 15 minutes
Serving size: 4 people

Ingredients:
400g fresh yellowtail fillet, thinly sliced
1 orange, juiced
1 lemon, juiced
1 lime, juiced
1 tbsp soy sauce
1 tsp mirin
1 tsp sesame oil
1 small red chili, finely sliced
1 tbsp fresh cilantro, chopped
Sea salt, to taste
Freshly ground black pepper, to taste
Microgreens, for garnish

Instructions:

Alright, let's begin this journey. First, ensure your yellowtail is as fresh as a morning breeze over the Tsukiji Fish Market. Slice the fillet into thin, delicate pieces and lay them out on a chilled plate.

Now, in a small bowl, combine the juices of the orange, lemon, and lime. This citrus trio will dance harmoniously on your palate. Add the soy sauce, mirin, and sesame oil to the mix. Stir gently but with purpose; this is your marinade.

Drizzle this zesty concoction over the yellowtail slices, making sure each piece gets its fair share of love. Don't rush—let the fish bask in the citrus symphony for about 5 minutes.

While the yellowtail is marinating, slice the red chili thinly and chop the fresh cilantro. These will add a vibrant kick and a splash of color to our dish.

Once marinated, arrange the yellowtail slices on a clean plate with the grace of a calligrapher's brushstroke. Sprinkle the red chili and cilantro over the top. Season lightly with sea salt and freshly ground black pepper.

Finally, for that touch of elegance, garnish with a few microgreens. They're like the cherry blossoms on a spring day—subtle, yet unforgettable.

Ah, there it is, a masterpiece of simplicity and flavor. Imagine the smiles and nods of approval as you serve this at your next gathering. Remember, in the world of sushi, sometimes less is more. Enjoy this citrusy delight, and may it bring joy to your table.

14. Octopus Carpaccio: Thinly Sliced Elegance

The octopus, often a mystery of the deep, transforms into a delicate masterpiece on your plate. This dish, with its tender, paper-thin slices, is like a symphony of the ocean—it sings, it dances, and it leaves you mesmerized with every bite.

Preparation time: 30 minutes
Cooking time: 1 hour
Ready-in time: 1 hour 30 minutes
Serving size: 4 people

Ingredients:
1 whole octopus (about 2 pounds)
1 cup white wine
2 bay leaves
1 lemon, sliced
1 teaspoon black peppercorns
1 teaspoon sea salt
1 cup ice water
2 tablespoons extra virgin olive oil
1 tablespoon yuzu juice
1 tablespoon soy sauce
Microgreens, for garnish
Thinly sliced radishes, for garnish

Instructions:

First, let's bring the octopus to life. In a large pot, combine the white wine, bay leaves, lemon slices, black peppercorns, and sea salt. Fill the pot with water and bring it to a boil over medium-high heat. Once boiling, carefully add the octopus and reduce the heat to a simmer. Cook the octopus for about 45 minutes to an hour until it becomes tender.

When the octopus is tender, transfer it to an ice water bath to stop the cooking process and to firm up the flesh. Let it cool for about 15 minutes. This step is crucial for achieving those perfect, paper-thin slices.

Now, let's make the octopus shine. Slice the cooled octopus as thinly as possible. A sharp knife is your best friend here. Arrange the slices in a single layer on a large serving platter.

In a small bowl, whisk together the olive oil, yuzu juice, and soy sauce. This dressing will add a fragrant, citrusy note that complements the octopus beautifully. Drizzle the dressing over the arranged octopus slices.

For the final touch, garnish with microgreens and thinly sliced radishes. The radishes add a peppery crunch, while the microgreens bring a fresh, herbal note. This dish is all about balance and harmony, much like a perfectly composed piece of music.

"Take a moment to admire your creation. You've turned the mysterious octopus into a work of art that belongs in a gallery. As you share this with friends and family, know that you've captured the essence of the ocean in every bite. Until next time, keep your knives sharp and your flavors bold!"

15. Scallop Sashimi: Sweet Ocean Freshness

Imagine the taste of the sea, delicate and silky, melting on your tongue. That's what awaits you in this delightful dish. Let's embark on a journey to the heart of the ocean, right from your kitchen.

Preparation time: 15 minutes
Cooking time: 0 minutes
Ready-in time: 15 minutes
Serving size: 4 people

Ingredients:
Fresh scallops, 12 large
Lemon zest, 1 teaspoon
Sea salt, 1 teaspoon
Soy sauce, 1 tablespoon
Wasabi, a small dab for each slice
Shiso leaves, 8 leaves
Microgreens, for garnish
Freshly ground black pepper, to taste

Instructions:

First, we must honor the star of our dish: the scallops. Carefully rinse them under cold water and pat them dry with a paper towel. Now, slice each scallop horizontally into thin, even pieces. Take your time—precision is key.

Next, place the scallop slices on a chilled plate, arranging them in a beautiful, fanned-out pattern. Presentation is everything; make it look like a work of art.

Sprinkle the lemon zest and sea salt gently over the scallop slices. This will enhance their natural sweetness and bring out the flavors of the ocean.

Add a small dab of wasabi to each slice of scallop. Remember, a little goes a long way. You want just enough to give a hint of heat without overpowering the delicate flavor of the scallops.

Drizzle the soy sauce over the scallops, ensuring each slice gets a touch of that umami richness. If you have a dropper, even better—precision is everything.

Carefully place a shiso leaf underneath each slice of scallop. The shiso's minty, slightly bitter taste provides a perfect contrast to the sweet, tender scallops.

Garnish with microgreens and a light sprinkle of freshly ground black pepper. These finishing touches will add a burst of color and a hint of spice, making your dish as visually stunning as it is delicious.

And there you have it—scallop sashimi that captures the essence of the sea, brought to life in your kitchen. Serve immediately and enjoy the sweet ocean freshness.

This dish is like a whisper from the sea, a reminder of nature's delicate beauty. Share it with those who appreciate the finer things in life, and let the flavors transport you to the ocean's embrace.

16. Toro Temptation: Fatty Tuna Indulgence

Imagine a delicate dance of flavors where the buttery richness of toro meets a symphony of subtle, vibrant ingredients. This is sushi at its most luxurious, a true testament to the art of indulgence.

Preparation time: 30 minutes
Cooking time: 10 minutes
Ready-in time: 40 minutes
Serving size: 4 people

Ingredients:
300 grams of toro (fatty tuna), sliced into thin pieces
2 cups of sushi rice, cooked and seasoned
4 sheets of nori (seaweed)
1 small cucumber, julienned
1 avocado, thinly sliced
2 tablespoons of tobiko (flying fish roe)
Soy sauce for dipping
Pickled ginger for garnish
Wasabi for serving

Instructions:

Alright, let's get started! First, you want to have your sushi rice cooked and seasoned. If you haven't done this yet, get that going because it needs to cool to room temperature.

While the rice is cooking, prepare the rest of your ingredients. Slice the toro into thin, luscious pieces, almost like you're cutting through butter. Next, julienne the cucumber into matchstick-sized pieces and thinly slice the avocado.

Now it's time to assemble. Lay a sheet of nori on your bamboo sushi mat, shiny side down. Wet your hands to prevent the rice from sticking, and spread a thin, even layer of sushi rice over the nori, leaving about an inch at the top free of rice.

Place a few slices of cucumber and avocado horizontally across the center of the rice. Then, lay several slices of the rich, fatty toro on top of the veggies. Sprinkle a bit of tobiko over the toro for that delightful crunch and pop.

Roll the sushi tightly using the bamboo mat, applying even pressure to shape it into a firm cylinder. Take your time here, and don't rush – this is the heart of the indulgence. Once rolled, use a sharp knife to cut the roll into bite-sized pieces. Wet the knife between cuts to ensure clean slices.

Arrange your rolls on a platter, and serve them with soy sauce, pickled ginger, and a touch of wasabi on the side.

Indulge in the luxurious flavors with each bite, savoring the richness that only toro can offer. Remember, sushi is more than just food – it's an experience, a celebration. Until our next culinary adventure, keep your knives sharp and your flavors bold!

17. Whitefish Sashimi: Delicate and Mild

In the heart of simplicity lies the beauty of whitefish sashimi. A symphony of flavors and textures that dances on your palate, transforming the mundane into the extraordinary.

Preparation time: 20 minutes
Cooking time: 0 minutes
Ready-in time: 20 minutes
Serving size: 4 people

Ingredients:
300 grams of fresh whitefish (flounder, sea bass, or snapper)
1 tablespoon of freshly grated wasabi
1 lemon, thinly sliced
1 tablespoon of finely chopped chives
2 sheets of shiso leaves, thinly sliced
Soy sauce for dipping
Microgreens for garnish

Instructions:

First, ensure your whitefish is incredibly fresh. The ocean's essence should still linger when you unwrap it. Slice the whitefish into thin, delicate pieces—each slice should be about the thickness of a playing card. Precision is key here; take your time and let your knife do the talking.

Next, arrange the slices artfully on a chilled plate. Think of it as painting with fish; the presentation should be as exquisite as the taste. Place a small mound of freshly grated wasabi to the side of the plate. The wasabi's fiery kick will complement the mildness of the fish beautifully.

Now, drape the thin lemon slices over the whitefish. The citrus will enhance the fish's delicate flavor, adding a touch of brightness and zest. Sprinkle the finely chopped chives and shiso leaves over the top. These herbs will provide a subtle, aromatic lift to each bite.

For the finishing touch, pour a small amount of soy sauce into a dipping bowl. The soy's umami depth will marry perfectly with the fish's lightness. Garnish with a few sprigs of microgreens to add a pop of color and a hint of earthiness.

As you serve, remind your guests to dip each piece lightly into the soy sauce, savoring the interplay of flavors and textures. The whitefish sashimi should be enjoyed slowly, allowing its delicate nuances to unfold on the palate.

Creating whitefish sashimi is like crafting a haiku—simple yet profound. May each bite transport you to a serene, coastal landscape where the sea's whispers linger on the breeze. Enjoy this delicate dance of flavors and let it inspire your culinary journey!

18. Squid Sensation: Tender and Fresh

Ah, the ocean's mysteries come alive in your hands, my friends! Today, we explore the delicate dance of flavor and texture with our star—squid— perfectly tender and oh-so-fresh.

Preparation time: 30 minutes
Cooking time: 10 minutes
Ready-in time: 40 minutes
Serving size: 4 people

Ingredients:
- 2 medium squid, cleaned and cut into rings
- 1 cup sushi rice
- 1 1/2 cups water
- 2 tablespoons rice vinegar
- 1 tablespoon sugar
- 1 teaspoon salt
- 1 avocado, thinly sliced
- 1 cucumber, julienned
- 1 tablespoon wasabi paste
- 4 sheets nori (seaweed)
- Soy sauce for dipping

Instructions:

First, my friends, let's prepare the sushi rice. Rinse the sushi rice under cold water until the water runs clear. Combine the rice and water in a rice cooker, and let it work its magic. Once cooked, fold in the rice vinegar, sugar, and salt. Let the rice cool, but not too much—we want it warm and fluffy.

Next, the squid. Heat a pot of water to a gentle boil. Add the squid rings and cook them for just about 2 minutes. They should be tender but still have a slight bite. Drain and set aside to cool.

Now, lay a sheet of nori on your bamboo mat, shiny side down. Wet your hands and spread a thin layer of sushi rice over the nori, leaving a small border at the top. Dab a line of wasabi across the center. Arrange a few slices of avocado, cucumber, and squid rings over the wasabi.

Time to roll! Carefully lift the edge of the mat and roll it over the filling, pressing gently but firmly. Keep rolling until you reach the border. Wet the edge of the nori with a bit of water and seal the roll. Repeat with the remaining ingredients.

Once all rolls are done, slice them into bite-sized pieces with a sharp knife. Serve with soy sauce for dipping, and let each bite transport you to the coastal shores of Japan.

Ah, the satisfaction of creating something beautiful and delicious with your own hands! May your journey in sushi-making be filled with joy and discovery. Until next time, keep your knives sharp and your flavors bold.

19. Mackerel Magic: Bold and Rich

In the hustle and bustle of life, there's a serene art in crafting sushi. Today, we bring the ocean to your table with a dish that captures the essence of the sea in every bite. Let's dive into the delicious depths of Mackerel Magic!

Preparation time: 30 minutes
Cooking time: 10 minutes
Ready-in time: 40 minutes
Serving size: 4 people

Ingredients:
2 fresh mackerel fillets
3 cups sushi rice, cooked and seasoned
1/2 cup rice vinegar
1 tablespoon soy sauce
1 tablespoon mirin
1 teaspoon grated ginger
1 teaspoon wasabi paste
4 sheets nori seaweed
1 small cucumber, julienned
1 avocado, thinly sliced
Pickled ginger, for serving
Soy sauce, for serving

Instructions:

First, let's get that mackerel ready. Rinse the fillets under cold water and pat them dry with paper towels. Lay them skin side up on a cutting board and, using a sharp knife, score the skin lightly in a crisscross pattern. This helps the flavors seep in beautifully.

In a small bowl, mix together the rice vinegar, soy sauce, mirin, and grated ginger. Place the mackerel fillets in a shallow dish and pour this savory mixture over them. Let the mackerel marinate for about 10 minutes, allowing it to absorb those bold, rich flavors.

While the mackerel is marinating, prepare your sushi rice. Make sure it's seasoned just right with a balance of rice vinegar, sugar, and salt. Spread the rice evenly over the nori sheets, leaving a small border at the top for sealing.

Now, it's time to assemble. Lay a marinated mackerel fillet on the edge of the rice-covered nori. Add a touch of wasabi paste, then arrange a few slices of cucumber and avocado alongside. Carefully roll the nori, using a bamboo mat if you have one, pressing gently to keep it all together.

Once rolled, use a sharp knife dipped in water to slice the roll into bite-sized pieces. Repeat the process with the remaining ingredients. Serve your mackerel sushi with pickled ginger and soy sauce on the side.

"Ah, the beauty of sushi! Each bite of this Mackerel Magic transports you to the heart of the ocean, a symphony of flavors dancing on your palate. Until next time, may your culinary adventures be as boundless as the sea!"

20. Sea Bream Slices: Subtle Sweetness

Imagine the serenity of the ocean, the crisp breeze, and the whisper of waves. Now, capture that essence on a plate with our Sea Bream Slices, where subtleness meets sweetness in perfect harmony.

Preparation time: 20 minutes
Cooking time: 10 minutes
Ready-in time: 30 minutes
Serving size: 4 people

Ingredients:
4 fresh sea bream fillets (about 150g each)
2 tablespoons soy sauce
1 tablespoon mirin
1 teaspoon sake
1 teaspoon sugar
1-inch piece of fresh ginger, thinly sliced
2 tablespoons finely chopped green onions
1 lemon, thinly sliced
A pinch of sea salt
A dash of sesame oil

Instructions:

Alright, let's embark on this culinary journey! Start by taking those beautiful sea bream fillets and giving them a gentle rinse under cold water. Pat them dry with a paper towel and lay them on a clean cutting board. Sprinkle a pinch of sea salt over the fillets, just a light dusting to enhance the natural flavors.

Next, grab a small mixing bowl. Pour in the soy sauce, mirin, sake, and sugar. Stir it all together until that sugar is fully dissolved. Now, the magic begins. Place the fillets in a shallow dish and pour this delightful marinade over them. Let the sea bream bathe in these flavors for about 10 minutes. Meanwhile, slice your ginger and lemon, and chop those green onions nice and fine.

Heat a dash of sesame oil in a non-stick skillet over medium heat. When the oil is shimmering, add the ginger slices. Let them sizzle for a moment, releasing their aromatic essence. Gently place the marinated sea bream fillets in the skillet, skin-side down. Cook for about 4 minutes, then carefully flip and cook for another 3 minutes.

As the fillets are finishing up, toss in those lemon slices for a quick sauté, just enough to soften them and release their bright, citrusy notes. Once ready, transfer the fillets to a serving plate, arranging the lemon slices on top and sprinkling the green onions over for that final touch.

And there you have it, a dish that's as light and refreshing as a summer sea breeze.

Ah, the Sea Bream Slices, a symphony of subtlety and sweetness that dances on your taste buds. Savor each bite, and let it transport you to the tranquil shores of culinary bliss. Until next time, happy cooking and even happier eating!

21. Classic Maguro Nigiri: Tuna Simplicity

In the heart of simplicity lies the true essence of sushi. Imagine tuna so fresh it seems to dance across your tongue. Welcome to the world of Maguro Nigiri, where elegance meets tradition, and every bite tells a story.

Preparation time: 20 minutes
Cooking time: 20 minutes
Ready-in time: 40 minutes
Serving size: 4 people

Ingredients:
2 cups sushi rice
2 1/2 cups water
1/4 cup rice vinegar
2 tablespoons sugar
1 teaspoon salt
8 slices fresh maguro (tuna), about 1/4-inch thick
Wasabi paste
Soy sauce, for serving
Pickled ginger, for serving

Instructions:

Let's start with the rice, the soul of sushi. Rinse the sushi rice until the water runs clear. This step is crucial to achieving that perfect, sticky texture. Once rinsed, combine the rice and water in a rice cooker and let it do its magic.

While the rice is cooking, mix together the rice vinegar, sugar, and salt in a small bowl until everything dissolves. This mixture will give our rice that sushi flavor.

When the rice is done, transfer it to a large bowl and gently fold in the vinegar mixture. Use a cutting motion with your rice paddle to avoid mashing the grains. Let it cool to room temperature – patience here will reward you with perfect nigiri.

Now, let's move on to the star of the show: maguro. Ensure your knife is sharp – a clean cut is essential for presentation and texture. Slice the tuna into eight even pieces, about 1/4-inch thick. Each slice should be delicate yet substantial.

Wet your hands with a mixture of water and rice vinegar to prevent the rice from sticking. Take a small amount of rice, about the size of a golf ball, and shape it into an oval. Place a dab of wasabi on one side of the tuna slice, then press the rice gently onto the wasabi side.

Turn the nigiri over so the tuna is on top, and press gently with your fingers to meld the fish and rice together. Repeat with the remaining slices.

Serve your maguro nigiri with soy sauce and pickled ginger on the side. Each bite should be a harmonious blend of flavors, simplicity itself yet profoundly satisfying.

Mastery is in the details, and you've just crafted a masterpiece. Remember, sushi isn't just food; it's an experience, a moment of zen with every bite. Enjoy your journey, and may your sushi always be perfect!

22. Eel Obsession: Unagi Nigiri

There's a certain magic in the delicate balance between sweet and savory that unagi brings to the table. This dish is not merely food; it's an experience. Let's embark on this flavorful adventure together, transforming simple ingredients into a symphony of taste.

Preparation time: 20 minutes
Cooking time: 15 minutes
Ready-in time: 35 minutes
Serving size: 4 people

Ingredients:
2 unagi (freshwater eel fillets, pre-cooked)
4 cups sushi rice, cooked
1/4 cup unagi sauce (store-bought or homemade)
2 tablespoons mirin
2 tablespoons soy sauce
1 tablespoon sugar
Wasabi, as needed
Pickled ginger, for serving

Instructions:

Alright, gather around! First, let's get our sushi rice ready. You should already have it cooked to perfection. If you need a refresher, remember: rinse the rice until the water runs clear, cook it with just the right amount of water, and season it with a mixture of rice vinegar, sugar, and salt. Let it cool to a manageable temperature.

Next, let's prepare the unagi. If you're using pre-cooked eel, you're halfway there! Mix the unagi sauce, mirin, soy sauce, and sugar in a small saucepan. Bring it to a gentle simmer over medium heat, stirring occasionally until it thickens slightly. Remove from heat and let it cool down.

Brush the unagi fillets generously with this glossy unagi sauce. Place them on a baking sheet lined with foil, and broil for about 5-7 minutes until they're caramelized and slightly crisp on the edges.

While your eel is broiling, let's shape the nigiri. Wet your hands with a little bit of water to prevent the rice from sticking. Grab a small handful of sushi rice, about the size of a ping-pong ball. Gently press and form it into an oval shape, firm but not squashed.

Once your unagi is ready, cut the fillets into bite-sized pieces that can rest comfortably atop your rice ovals. Add a tiny dab of wasabi on top of each rice mound. This will act as a glue and add a hint of heat.

Now, place a piece of unagi on top of each rice mound, pressing gently to secure it. Brush a little more unagi sauce on top for that extra sheen and flavor boost.

Serve your unagi nigiri with pickled ginger on the side, and maybe a touch more wasabi if you're feeling adventurous.

And there you have it, a dish worthy of admiration and delight! Remember, each bite tells a story, so savor the journey and share the experience. Until our next culinary adventure, keep your knives sharp and your hearts full!

23. Hamachi Harmony: Yellowtail Nigiri

Imagine the ocean breeze, the waves softly crashing, and the delicate balance of flavors that dance on your palate. This is what you'll create with Hamachi Harmony: Yellowtail Nigiri.

Preparation time: 30 minutes
Cooking time: 15 minutes
Ready-in time: 45 minutes
Serving size: 4 people

Ingredients:
300 grams sushi-grade yellowtail (hamachi), thinly sliced
2 cups sushi rice, cooked and cooled
4 tablespoons rice vinegar
2 tablespoons sugar
1 teaspoon salt
Wasabi, to taste
Soy sauce, for serving
Pickled ginger (gari), for serving

Instructions:

First, let's prepare the sushi rice. In a small bowl, mix the rice vinegar, sugar, and salt until fully dissolved. Drizzle this seasoned vinegar over your cooked sushi rice, folding gently to combine. Be mindful not to mash the rice; we want each grain to stand proudly.

Next, slice your sushi-grade yellowtail into thin, elegant pieces. Each slice should be about two fingers wide and one bite perfect. This is where your knife skills shine, so take your time and enjoy the process.

Now, it's time to form the nigiri. Moisten your hands with a bit of water to prevent sticking, then take a small portion of rice (about the size of a ping-pong ball) and gently shape it into an oval. Don't compress it too hard; the rice should be firm but airy.

Take a dab of wasabi and spread it lightly on one side of the yellowtail slice. Place the yellowtail, wasabi side down, on top of the rice. Gently press the fish and rice together, ensuring they bond without squishing the rice.

Repeat this process until all your yellowtail and rice have partnered up in delightful harmony. Arrange your nigiri on a beautiful plate, serving with soy sauce and pickled ginger on the side.

"Ah, the masterpiece is complete! Savor the delicate harmony of flavors, and let the ocean's melody play on your taste buds. Until next time, keep your knives sharp and your heart full of culinary passion."

24. Ikura Explosion: Salmon Roe Nigiri

Imagine the burst of the ocean's essence on your palate, a cascade of briny pearls that invigorate the senses. This dish is a celebration of simplicity and purity, capturing the very soul of the sea in each bite.

Preparation time: 20 minutes
Cooking time: 10 minutes
Ready-in time: 30 minutes
Serving size: 4 people

Ingredients:
Sushi rice - 2 cups
Water - 2 1/2 cups
Rice vinegar - 1/4 cup
Sugar - 2 tablespoons
Salt - 1 teaspoon
Salmon roe (Ikura) - 1 cup
Nori seaweed - 1 sheet, cut into thin strips
Wasabi - as needed
Soy sauce - for serving

Instructions:

First, let's start with our sushi rice. Rinse the rice under cold water until the water runs clear. This step is crucial to remove excess starch and achieve that perfect sticky texture. Once rinsed, combine the rice and water in a rice cooker and let it do its magic. If you don't have a rice cooker, simply bring the rice and water to a boil in a pot, then cover, reduce the heat to low, and simmer for about 15 minutes.

While your rice is cooking, let's prepare the sushi vinegar. In a small saucepan, combine the rice vinegar, sugar, and salt. Heat gently until the sugar and salt dissolve completely. Set aside to cool.

Once the rice is cooked, transfer it to a large bowl. Gently fold in the sushi vinegar mixture using a wooden spatula. Be careful not to mash the rice—treat it like a delicate treasure. Allow the seasoned rice to cool until it's just warm to the touch.

Now, it's time to shape your nigiri. Wet your hands with a mixture of water and rice vinegar to prevent sticking. Take a small handful of rice and form it into an oval shape, about the size of two fingers. Repeat this process until you have the desired number of rice bases.

Next, place a small amount of wasabi on top of each rice oval. This will act as a natural adhesive and introduce a subtle kick to balance the richness of the roe.

Gently spoon a generous amount of salmon roe onto each piece of rice. Top with a thin strip of nori to hold the ikura in place, adding a touch of elegance and authenticity to your nigiri.

Serve your Ikura Explosion Nigiri with soy sauce on the side. Each bite promises an explosion of flavors, bringing the ocean's bounty straight to your table.

Bravo, sushi aficionados! You've just mastered a dish that brings the ocean's essence to your plate with elegance and flair. Now, each bite is a celebration of culinary artistry. Enjoy this moment, and remember, the journey to sushi mastery is as delightful as each savory bite!

25. Sweet Shrimp Nigiri: Amaebi Delight

Ah, the sweet shrimp, or amaebi, is a treasure of the sea. Its delicate sweetness and tender texture are like a whisper of the ocean on your palate. This dish is a symphony of simplicity and elegance, perfect for a special occasion or a serene evening at home.

Preparation time: 20 minutes
Cooking time: 10 minutes
Ready-in time: 30 minutes
Serving size: 4 people

Ingredients:
2 cups sushi rice
2 1/2 cups water
1/4 cup rice vinegar
2 tablespoons sugar
1 teaspoon salt
16 amaebi (sweet shrimp), cleaned and peeled
Wasabi paste
Soy sauce, for serving
Pickled ginger, for serving

Instructions:

Let's embark on this culinary journey together. First, rinse the sushi rice under cold water until the water runs clear. This step is crucial for removing excess starch and achieving that perfect sticky texture. Now, combine the rice with 2 1/2 cups of water in a rice cooker or a pot. Cook until the rice is fluffy and tender, just like a cloud on a summer day.

While the rice is cooking, let's prepare the sushi vinegar. In a small saucepan, gently heat the rice vinegar with sugar and salt until dissolved. Remove from heat and let it cool. Once your rice is ready, transfer it to a wooden or non-metallic bowl. Gradually fold in the sushi vinegar mixture, being careful not to smash the grains. Let the seasoned rice cool to room temperature under a damp cloth.

Time to bring out the stars of our show, the amaebi. Carefully peel and clean the sweet shrimp, keeping the tails intact for that elegant presentation. If you're feeling adventurous, you can even deep-fry the shrimp heads for a crunchy treat on the side.

With wet hands, form small, oblong mounds of sushi rice, about the size of a golf ball. Dab a small amount of wasabi on top of each rice mound. Gently press an amaebi onto each rice ball, allowing the natural sweetness of the shrimp to meld with the vinegared rice.

Arrange your sweet shrimp nigiri on a beautiful platter. Serve with soy sauce and pickled ginger on the side, allowing each bite to be a harmonious dance of flavors.

Ah, the amaebi delight! Each piece is a little love letter from the sea, wrapped in a tender embrace of rice. Enjoy this moment, and let the delicate sweetness transport you to a serene seaside. Until next time, may your culinary adventures be ever flavorful and joyous.

26. Snapper Surprise: Tai Nigiri

When it comes to sushi, the element of surprise is essential. Imagine the subtle sweetness of snapper, melting into your taste buds, as the perfect bite of rice holds it together. Let's craft this symphony of flavors with the utmost precision and care.

Preparation time: 20 minutes
Cooking time: 10 minutes
Ready-in time: 30 minutes
Serving size: 4 people

Ingredients:
1 cup sushi rice
1 1/4 cups water
1/4 cup rice vinegar
2 tablespoons sugar
1/2 teaspoon salt
8 slices of fresh snapper (Tai) fillet
Wasabi paste
Soy sauce for serving
Pickled ginger for serving

Instructions:

First, let's prepare the sushi rice, which is the foundation of our nigiri. Rinse the sushi rice under cold water until the water runs clear. This step is crucial to remove excess starch. Combine the rice and water in a rice cooker, and let it steam until tender.

While the rice is cooking, mix together the rice vinegar, sugar, and salt in a small bowl until the sugar and salt dissolve. Once the rice is done, transfer it to a large bowl and gently fold in the vinegar mixture. Try not to mash the grains—gentleness is key here.

Next, let's move to the star of our dish: the snapper. Ensure your snapper slices are thin and uniform. This will ensure an even experience with each bite. Take a small amount of wasabi and spread it onto each slice of snapper. Wasabi isn't just spicy—it's aromatic and elevates the fish's natural flavor.

Now, with wet hands, form the sushi rice into bite-sized mounds. Think of shaping a small log about the size of two fingers. Place each slice of snapper over the rice, pressing gently to secure it. The snapper should drape over the rice like a luxurious blanket.

Serve your Tai Nigiri with soy sauce and pickled ginger on the side. The soy sauce adds a salty depth, while the pickled ginger cleanses the palate between bites, preparing you for the next delightful surprise.

Bravo, sushi maestro! You've just crafted a dish that sings with the essence of the sea. Remember, in sushi, every detail matters, and you've handled them with grace. Until next time, keep your knives sharp and your creativity sharper!

27. Seared Salmon Nigiri: Torched Flavor

Imagine the subtle dance of the sea brought to your plate, where the tender salmon meets the fiery kiss of a blowtorch, creating an unforgettable symphony of flavors.

Preparation time: 20 minutes
Cooking time: 5 minutes
Ready-in time: 25 minutes
Serving size: 4 people

Ingredients:
300 grams of sushi-grade salmon fillet, sliced into 8 pieces
2 cups of sushi rice, cooked and seasoned with rice vinegar
1 tablespoon soy sauce
1 tablespoon mirin
1 teaspoon sugar
1 tablespoon of wasabi
8 thin slices of pickled ginger
Toasted sesame seeds for garnish
Fresh chives for garnish

Instructions:

First, let's prepare the sushi rice. You've got your perfectly cooked sushi rice, right? Fluffy and seasoned just right with a blend of rice vinegar, a hint of sugar, and a touch of salt. Now, wet your hands – this is crucial to avoid the sticky mess! Grab a small handful of rice, shaping it gently into an oblong mound, about the size of a quail egg. Repeat this process until you have eight rice mounds.

Next, take your sushi-grade salmon fillet. Slice it into eight pieces, each about the thickness of your pinky finger. Lay each slice of salmon over the rice mounds, pressing down lightly to adhere.

In a small bowl, mix together the soy sauce, mirin, and sugar until the sugar dissolves. Using a brush, lightly glaze the top of each salmon slice with this delightful mixture. This is where the magic begins.

Now, for the fun part – torching! If you've never used a culinary blowtorch before, don't be shy. Hold the torch about 2-3 inches away from the fish, and gently sear the top of the salmon until it's slightly charred. You'll see the edges curl and the surface caramelize beautifully, releasing an irresistible aroma.

Once seared, place a small dab of wasabi between the salmon and the rice for that extra kick. Garnish each piece with a thin slice of pickled ginger, a sprinkle of toasted sesame seeds, and a few finely chopped chives. Voilà! Your Seared Salmon Nigiri is ready to dazzle.

Remember, each bite of this seared creation is a step into a world where tradition meets innovation. Savor every moment, and let the flavors tell you their story. Until next time, keep your knives sharp and your spirits high!

28. Tamago Nigiri: Sweet Egg on Rice

Imagine a delicate dance of flavors, where the sweet and savory waltz together on a bed of perfectly seasoned rice. This is Tamago Nigiri, a humble yet sophisticated bite that will transport you to the heart of Japanese culinary tradition.

Preparation time: 15 minutes
Cooking time: 30 minutes
Ready-in time: 45 minutes
Serving size: 4 people

Ingredients:
6 large eggs
2 tablespoons sugar
1 teaspoon mirin
1 teaspoon soy sauce
1 teaspoon dashi stock
2 cups sushi rice, cooked and seasoned
1 sheet nori, cut into thin strips
Soy sauce and pickled ginger, for serving

Instructions:

Alright, let's get started! First, crack those eggs into a bowl and give them a good whisk until they're beautifully blended. Add your sugar, mirin, soy sauce, and dashi stock to the mix, and whisk again until everything is well incorporated. We want this mixture to be smooth and harmonious.

Now, heat a rectangular tamagoyaki pan over medium heat, and lightly oil it. If you don't have a tamagoyaki pan, a small non-stick skillet will do just fine. Pour a thin layer of your egg mixture into the pan, tilting it to cover the bottom evenly. Let it cook until it's just set but not browned.

Carefully roll the egg from one end of the pan to the other using a spatula or chopsticks. After you've made your first roll, push it to the side of the pan. Add another thin layer of egg mixture, lifting your first roll to let the uncooked egg flow underneath. Once this new layer is set, roll it together with your first roll. Repeat this process until all the egg mixture is used up and you have a lovely, layered omelet.

Transfer your tamagoyaki to a bamboo mat or a clean towel, and shape it into a neat rectangle while it's still hot. Let it cool slightly before slicing it into 8 even pieces.

Next, wet your hands with water to prevent sticking, and form small, oblong mounds of sushi rice. Each should be about the size of a golf ball. Place a slice of tamagoyaki on top of each mound of rice, and secure it with a strip of nori.

Serve your Tamago Nigiri with a little soy sauce and pickled ginger on the side. Enjoy the delightful contrast of the sweet egg and seasoned rice.

Bravo! You have just crafted a classic Tamago Nigiri, a testament to the beauty of simplicity in Japanese cuisine. Let each bite remind you of the elegance of traditional flavors, and share this experience with those you cherish. Until next time, keep mastering the art of sushi!

29. Wasabi Infused Nigiri: A Spicy Twist

Ah, the art of sushi! It's not just about the fish or the rice, but the magic in the balance, the harmony of flavors. Today, we add a fiery dance partner to our sushi symphony—wasabi.

Preparation time: 20 minutes
Cooking time: 15 minutes
Ready-in time: 35 minutes
Serving size: 4 people

Ingredients:
2 cups sushi rice
2 ½ cups water
¼ cup rice vinegar
2 tablespoons sugar
1 teaspoon salt
12-16 slices of fresh sashimi-grade fish (tuna, salmon, yellowtail)
2 tablespoons wasabi paste
Soy sauce for dipping
Pickled ginger for serving
Nori (optional, for garnish)

Instructions:

First, let's get that rice perfect. Rinse the sushi rice under cold water until the water runs clear. We need clarity in our sushi, just like in life. Combine the rinsed rice and water in a rice cooker. Let it cook—no peeking!

While the rice is doing its thing, let's prep the vinegar mix. In a small saucepan, combine rice vinegar, sugar, and salt. Heat gently, just until the sugar dissolves. This is the essence of balance—sweet and salty in perfect harmony. Remove from heat and let it cool.

Once the rice is done, transfer it to a large bowl. Gently fold in the vinegar mixture with a wooden spoon or rice paddle. Be gentle, like you're whispering to the rice. Let it cool to room temperature.

Now, the star of our show—wasabi! Take your wasabi paste and gently rub a small amount onto each slice of fish. Wasabi is powerful, so a little goes a long way. Imagine you're painting a delicate masterpiece.

Time to shape the rice. Wet your hands with water to prevent sticking. Take a small amount of rice, about the size of a ping-pong ball, and shape it into an oval. Place a slice of wasabi-infused fish over the rice, pressing gently so it adheres. Repeat with the remaining rice and fish.

Arrange your wasabi-infused nigiri on a beautiful platter. Serve with soy sauce for dipping and pickled ginger on the side. A touch of nori can add that extra flair if you desire.

Ah, the fiery kiss of wasabi meets the tender embrace of sashimi. Each bite is a journey, a dance of flavors that tells a story. Enjoy this spicy twist on traditional nigiri, and remember, the joy of sushi lies in the balance and the adventure. Until next time, keep rolling!

30. Red Snapper Nigiri: Aka-Tai Delight

In the heart of every sushi lover lies a yearning for perfection. The Aka-Tai, with its vibrant hues and tender flesh, promises a culinary journey that dances on the palate. Let's embark on this flavorful adventure together!

Preparation time: 30 minutes
Cooking time: 20 minutes
Ready-in time: 50 minutes
Serving size: 4 people

Ingredients:
2 cups sushi rice
2 1/2 cups water
1/4 cup rice vinegar
2 tablespoons sugar
1 teaspoon salt
8 slices red snapper (Aka-Tai), about 1/4 inch thick
1 sheet nori, cut into thin strips
Wasabi, to taste
Soy sauce, for serving
Pickled ginger, for serving

Instructions:

First, we honor the rice. Rinse the sushi rice under cold water until the water runs clear. This is not just a rinse; it's a purification. Once cleansed, combine the rice with water in a rice cooker and let it do its magic.

While the rice is cooking, prepare the sushi vinegar. In a small saucepan, gently warm the rice vinegar, sugar, and salt until dissolved. No boiling! Just enough warmth to blend them into harmony. Set this aside to cool.

Now, the red snapper, our Aka-Tai. Ensure your slices are pristine and fresh. They should glisten like the morning sun on a calm sea. Lay them out and keep them cool and covered.

When the rice cooker finishes, transfer the hot rice to a large bowl. Slowly pour the sushi vinegar over the rice and fold it in with a wooden paddle. Be gentle, like you're caressing a delicate flower. Fan the rice as you mix to bring it to room temperature. This will give it that perfect shiny finish.

With your hands moistened, take a small amount of rice and shape it into a compact, elongated mound. Place a dab of wasabi on one side of the red snapper slice, then lay the fish, wasabi side down, onto the rice. Gently press to adhere.

For a touch of elegance, wrap a thin strip of nori around the center of each nigiri, securing the fish to the rice. This isn't just for looks; it's a hug from the sea!

Serve your Aka-Tai Nigiri with soy sauce and pickled ginger. Each bite should be a symphony of flavors—savory, sweet, and a hint of the ocean.

Like the gentle waves that kiss the shore, may this Aka-Tai delight bring peace and joy to your table. Remember, every grain of rice is a testament to your dedication. Until our next culinary adventure, keep your knives sharp and your heart open!

31. California Fusion Roll: West Meets East

Imagine blending the vibrant flavors of California with the timeless elegance of Japanese sushi. This fusion roll is a symphony of East and West, each bite a harmonious blend of textures and tastes that will transport you across the Pacific.

Preparation time: 30 minutes
Cooking time: 20 minutes
Ready-in time: 50 minutes
Serving size: 4 people

Ingredients:
2 cups sushi rice
2 1/2 cups water
1/2 cup rice vinegar
2 tablespoons sugar
2 teaspoons salt
4 nori sheets
1 avocado, sliced
1 cucumber, julienned
8 ounces cooked crab meat
2 tablespoons Japanese mayonnaise
1 tablespoon sriracha
1/2 cup masago (capelin roe)
1/4 cup pickled ginger
Soy sauce, for serving

Instructions:

Alright, let's embark on this culinary adventure! Start by rinsing the sushi rice under cold water until the water runs clear. Combine the rice and water in a rice cooker and let it do its magic. Once cooked, transfer the rice to a large bowl. Mix the rice vinegar, sugar, and salt in a small bowl until dissolved, then gently fold this mixture into the rice. Let it cool to room temperature.

Now for the fun part. Lay a bamboo sushi mat on a flat surface and cover it with plastic wrap. Place a nori sheet shiny side down on the mat. Wet your fingers to prevent sticking, and spread a thin layer of sushi rice over the nori, leaving a 1-inch border at the top.

Flip the nori over so the rice is facing down. Arrange a slice of avocado, a few cucumber sticks, and a portion of crab meat along the center of the nori. Mix the Japanese mayonnaise with sriracha and drizzle a little over the crab.

Using the bamboo mat, carefully roll the sushi away from you, pressing firmly to shape it into a cylinder. Once rolled, sprinkle the masago on top and gently press it into the rice.

Repeat the process for the remaining nori sheets. Use a sharp knife to slice each roll into 8 pieces. Serve the rolls beautifully arranged on a plate with a side of pickled ginger and soy sauce for dipping.

Bravo! You've just created a masterpiece that bridges two worlds. Enjoy each bite of your California Fusion Roll, and remember, the kitchen is your canvas – keep experimenting and let your culinary spirit soar!

32. Spicy Tuna Roll: Fiery Bites

In the heart of the sushi world, where tradition meets innovation, the Spicy Tuna Roll stands as a testament to fiery flavors and delicate artistry. Let's embark on a culinary journey that will ignite your taste buds and leave you craving for more.

Preparation time: 20 minutes
Cooking time: 10 minutes
Ready-in time: 30 minutes
Serving size: 4 people

Ingredients:
1 cup sushi rice
1 1/4 cups water
2 tablespoons rice vinegar
1 tablespoon sugar
1 teaspoon salt
200 grams fresh tuna, finely chopped
2 tablespoons sriracha sauce
1 tablespoon mayonnaise
4 sheets nori (seaweed)
1 avocado, sliced
1 cucumber, julienned
Soy sauce, for serving
Pickled ginger, for serving
Wasabi, for serving

Instructions:

First, let's get our rice ready. Combine the sushi rice and water in a rice cooker. Once it's cooked, let it cool and then gently fold in the rice vinegar, sugar, and salt. This mixture gives our sushi rice that perfect flavor balance.

Next, let's spice things up. In a bowl, mix the finely chopped tuna with sriracha sauce and mayonnaise. This fiery blend is what gives our roll its kick.

Lay out a bamboo sushi mat and place a sheet of plastic wrap over it. Then, place a sheet of nori on top. With wet hands, spread a thin, even layer of the seasoned rice over the nori, leaving a small border at the top.

Now, flip the nori and rice over so the rice is facing down. On the nori, arrange a line of the spicy tuna mixture, followed by a few slices of avocado and cucumber. Carefully roll it up, using the bamboo mat to shape it tightly.

Slice your roll into bite-sized pieces with a sharp, wet knife to prevent sticking. Serve with soy sauce, pickled ginger, and a dab of wasabi on the side.

"Congratulations, sushi master! You've crafted a roll that's not just food, but an experience. Enjoy these fiery bites and let your taste buds dance with delight. Until our next culinary adventure, keep rolling and keep those flavors bold!"

33. Dragon Roll: Eel and Avocado Harmony

Imagine a dragon soaring through the sky, its scales shimmering under the sun. This roll captures that majesty, bringing the rich, smoky flavors of eel together with the creamy decadence of avocado. A bite of this roll is like tasting a legend.

Preparation time: 20 minutes
Cooking time: 10 minutes
Ready-in time: 30 minutes
Serving size: 4 people

Ingredients:
2 cups sushi rice, cooked and seasoned
4 sheets nori (seaweed)
8 ounces grilled eel (unagi), sliced into strips
1 avocado, thinly sliced
1 cucumber, julienned
2 tablespoons unagi sauce
1 tablespoon sesame seeds
Wasabi, for serving
Pickled ginger, for serving
Soy sauce, for serving

Instructions:
Alright, let's get started! First, lay out your bamboo mat and cover it with plastic wrap. This trick will make rolling much easier and cleaner. Place a sheet of nori on the mat, shiny side down. Wet your hands to prevent sticking and spread a thin, even layer of sushi rice over the nori, leaving a small border at the top.

Next, flip the nori over so the rice is facing down. This is a fun maneuver, trust me. Now, arrange a few strips of grilled eel along the center of the nori, followed by a line of cucumber julienne for that crisp bite.

Here's where the magic happens: carefully roll the sushi using the bamboo mat, pressing gently but firmly to shape it into a tight cylinder. The rice should be on the outside, encasing the eel and cucumber.

Once your roll is formed, take those beautiful avocado slices and drape them over the top. Use a piece of plastic wrap to help press the avocado gently onto the roll, ensuring it sticks. Sprinkle sesame seeds over the top for a bit of crunch and visual appeal.

Grab a sharp knife and slice the roll into eight equal pieces. A little tip: wet the knife with water before each cut for cleaner slices.

Drizzle unagi sauce over the top of the roll, adding that sweet, savory glaze that brings everything together. Serve your Dragon Roll with wasabi, pickled ginger, and soy sauce on the side.

There you have it – a masterpiece on a plate! This Dragon Roll will not only impress your guests but also transport them to a realm where flavors dance and dragons reign. Until next time, keep rolling and keep dreaming!

34. Rainbow Roll: A Colorful Feast

In the heart of every sushi roll lies a story, a tale woven with flavors and colors that captivate both the eyes and the palate. Today, we embark on a journey to create a vibrant masterpiece - the Rainbow Roll.

Preparation time: 30 minutes
Cooking time: 20 minutes
Ready-in time: 50 minutes
Serving size: 4 people

Ingredients:
2 cups sushi rice
2 1/2 cups water
1/4 cup rice vinegar
2 tablespoons sugar
1 teaspoon salt
4 sheets nori (seaweed)
1 avocado, thinly sliced
1 cucumber, julienned
8 ounces imitation crab meat
4 ounces ahi tuna, thinly sliced
4 ounces salmon, thinly sliced
4 ounces yellowtail, thinly sliced
1 tablespoon sesame seeds, toasted
Soy sauce, for serving
Pickled ginger, for serving
Wasabi, for serving

Instructions:

First, let's get that sushi rice ready. Rinse the sushi rice under cold water until the water runs clear. This step is crucial to achieve that perfect, sticky texture. Combine the rice and water in a rice cooker, and let it do its magic. Once cooked, transfer the rice to a large bowl. Mix the rice vinegar, sugar, and salt until dissolved, and gently fold this mixture into the warm rice. Let it cool to room temperature.

Now, the fun begins! Place a sheet of nori on your bamboo mat, shiny side down. Wet your hands with water to prevent sticking, and spread a thin, even layer of sushi rice over the nori, leaving about an inch at the top edge. Sprinkle those toasted sesame seeds over the rice for an extra layer of flavor.

Flip the nori over so that the rice is facing down. In the center of the nori, place a few slices of avocado, cucumber, and imitation crab meat. Carefully lift the edge of the bamboo mat closest to you, and begin rolling it away from you, pressing firmly but gently to keep the roll tight and even. Moisten the top edge of the nori with a bit of water to seal the roll.

Now, here comes the rainbow! Layer the thin slices of ahi tuna, salmon, and yellowtail across the top of the roll, alternating for that beautiful spectrum of colors. Cover the roll with plastic wrap and gently press to adhere the fish to the rice. Remove the plastic wrap and use a sharp knife dipped in water to slice the roll into eight even pieces.

Serve your Rainbow Roll with soy sauce, pickled ginger, and a dab of wasabi on the side.

Marvel at the mesmerizing hues of your creation, and savor each bite as it transports you to a world where flavors dance and colors sing. Remember, the art of sushi is a journey, and every roll is a step towards mastery. Enjoy!

35. Shrimp Tempura Roll: Crunchy Delight

In the heart of Tokyo, where every bite of sushi tells a story of tradition and innovation, the Shrimp Tempura Roll stands out as a testament to culinary artistry. Let's embark on this flavorful journey together, where crunch meets the delicate embrace of sushi rice and nori.

Preparation time: 25 minutes
Cooking time: 20 minutes
Ready-in time: 45 minutes
Serving size: 4 people

Ingredients:
2 cups sushi rice, cooked
2 tablespoons rice vinegar
1 tablespoon sugar
1 teaspoon salt
8 large shrimp, peeled and deveined
1 cup tempura batter mix
1/2 cup ice-cold water
1 avocado, thinly sliced
1 cucumber, julienned
4 sheets of nori (seaweed)
Vegetable oil, for frying
Soy sauce, for serving
Pickled ginger, for serving
Wasabi, for serving

Instructions:

First, let's start by preparing the sushi rice. While the rice is still warm, mix in the rice vinegar, sugar, and salt until well combined. Set it aside to cool to room temperature.

Next, let's turn our attention to the shrimp. Pat them dry with a paper towel, and then prepare the tempura batter by mixing the tempura batter mix with ice-cold water. The key here is to keep the batter light and airy, so don't overmix it.

Heat the vegetable oil in a deep fryer or a heavy-bottomed pot to 350°F (175°C). Dip each shrimp into the tempura batter, ensuring they are well-coated, and then carefully place them into the hot oil. Fry the shrimp until they are golden and crispy, about 2-3 minutes. Remove them from the oil and drain on a paper towel-lined plate.

Now, let's assemble the roll. Place a sheet of nori on a bamboo sushi mat, shiny side down. Wet your hands with a mixture of water and rice vinegar to prevent sticking, and then evenly spread a thin layer of sushi rice over the nori, leaving a 1-inch border at the top.

Place two pieces of the tempura shrimp horizontally across the center of the rice, followed by slices of avocado and cucumber. Carefully lift the edge of the bamboo mat closest to you, and begin rolling the sushi away from you, applying gentle pressure to ensure a tight roll. Seal the edge with the exposed strip of nori.

Using a sharp knife, cut the roll into 8 equal pieces. For the best results, clean the knife with a damp cloth between cuts. Arrange the pieces on a serving platter and serve with soy sauce, pickled ginger, and wasabi.

Ah, the symphony of crunch and tenderness in each bite of the Shrimp Tempura Roll! May your culinary adventure be as delightful as the first taste of this crunchy delight. Until our next sushi endeavor, savor the flavors and share the joy!

36. Philadelphia Roll: Cream Cheese Classic

Ah, the Philadelphia Roll! It's like a love letter to both Japan and the City of Brotherly Love. Imagine the velvety cream cheese embracing the delicate salmon, all wrapped up in a cozy blanket of nori and rice. Pure harmony, indeed.

Preparation time: 20 minutes
Cooking time: 15 minutes
Ready-in time: 35 minutes
Serving size: 4 people

Ingredients:
2 cups sushi rice
2 1/2 cups water
1/4 cup rice vinegar
2 tablespoons sugar
1 teaspoon salt
4 sheets nori (seaweed)
8 ounces smoked salmon
4 ounces cream cheese
1 small cucumber
1 avocado
Soy sauce for dipping
Pickled ginger for serving
Wasabi for serving

Instructions:

First, let's talk rice. Rinse your sushi rice under cold water until it runs clear. Place it into a rice cooker with 2 1/2 cups water. Once it's cooked, allow it to cool slightly. While it's cooling, mix together the rice vinegar, sugar, and salt until the sugar dissolves. Fold this mixture into your rice. Yes, fold it gently, like you're cradling a baby.

Now, let's move on to the stars of our roll. Slice the smoked salmon into thin strips. Do the same with the cream cheese; make sure it's chilled so it's easier to handle. Cut the cucumber into julienne strips and the avocado into thin slices.

Lay a sheet of nori on your bamboo mat, shiny side down. Wet your hands to prevent the rice from sticking, and spread a thin layer of rice over the nori, leaving about an inch at the top edge. Flip the nori so the rice side is down.

Place a few strips of smoked salmon, cream cheese, cucumber, and avocado in the center of the nori. Now, for the fun part—rolling! Using your bamboo mat, roll the nori over the fillings, pressing gently but firmly. Continue rolling until you reach the edge of the nori. Give it a gentle squeeze to shape.

Using a sharp knife dipped in water, slice the roll into 6-8 pieces. Clean the knife between cuts to keep everything neat.

Serve your Philadelphia Rolls with soy sauce, pickled ginger, and a dab of wasabi. Enjoy the symphony of flavors with each bite!

Ah, there you have it, the Philadelphia Roll! A bite of this, and you'll feel like you're standing on both sides of the world. Remember, sushi is not just food—it's an experience. Until next time, keep your knives sharp and your flavors sharper!

37. Salmon Avocado Roll: Creamy Perfection

In the delicate dance of sushi-making, few combinations strike a balance as elegantly as salmon and avocado. This roll captures the essence of creamy textures and fresh flavors, creating a symphony on your palate that you'll want to replay over and over.

Preparation time: 30 minutes
Cooking time: 20 minutes
Ready-in time: 50 minutes
Serving size: 4 people

Ingredients:
2 cups sushi rice
2 1/2 cups water
1/4 cup rice vinegar
2 tablespoons sugar
1 teaspoon salt
4 sheets nori (seaweed)
8 ounces fresh salmon, thinly sliced
2 ripe avocados, sliced
1 cucumber, julienned
2 tablespoons sesame seeds
Soy sauce, for serving
Pickled ginger, for serving
Wasabi, for serving

Instructions:

Alright, let's embark on this sushi adventure together. First, we'll start with the sushi rice. Rinse the rice under cold water until the water runs clear. Combine the rice and water in a rice cooker and let it do its magic. Once cooked, transfer the rice to a wooden or plastic bowl. Mix the rice vinegar, sugar, and salt in a small bowl until dissolved, then gently fold this mixture into the warm rice. Let it cool to room temperature.

Now, let's get our rolling station ready. Place a bamboo sushi mat on a clean surface and cover it with plastic wrap. Lay a sheet of nori, shiny side down, on the mat. Wet your hands to prevent the rice from sticking and spread a thin, even layer of rice over the nori, leaving about an inch at the top for sealing.

Sprinkle sesame seeds over the rice for that extra nutty crunch. Flip the nori and rice over so the rice side is down. Arrange a few slices of salmon, avocado, and cucumber along the center of the nori.

Time to roll! Using the bamboo mat, lift the edge closest to you and begin to roll the nori over the filling, pressing gently but firmly to keep it tight. Continue rolling until you reach the exposed edge of the nori. Wet the edge slightly to seal the roll.

With a sharp knife, cut the roll into 6-8 pieces. Repeat the process with the remaining ingredients until you have a beautiful array of salmon avocado rolls.

Serve your masterpiece with soy sauce, pickled ginger, and a dab of wasabi on the side. Enjoy the fruits of your labor!

"Congratulations, sushi artist! You've just crafted a roll that's as pleasing to the eye as it is to the taste buds. Remember, practice makes perfect, and each roll brings you closer to sushi mastery. Savor each bite and share this creamy perfection with those you love!"

38. Vegetable Roll: Garden Fresh

Imagine the first crisp bite into a vibrant garden wrapped in a delicate sheet of nori. This isn't just a vegetable roll; it's a celebration of nature's most colorful offerings, rolled up into a symphony of flavors that dance on your palate.

Preparation time: 30 minutes
Cooking time: 10 minutes
Ready-in time: 40 minutes
Serving size: 4 people

Ingredients:
2 cups sushi rice, cooked and cooled
3 tablespoons rice vinegar
2 tablespoons sugar
1 teaspoon salt
4 sheets nori (seaweed)
1 small cucumber, julienned
1 small carrot, julienned
1 ripe avocado, thinly sliced
1 red bell pepper, julienned
4 leaves of butter lettuce
1 tablespoon sesame seeds, toasted
Soy sauce, for serving
Pickled ginger, for serving
Wasabi, for serving

Instructions:

First, my friends, let's prepare our sushi rice. Combine the rice vinegar, sugar, and salt in a small bowl and stir until dissolved. Gently fold this mixture into the cooked sushi rice, ensuring each grain is lovingly coated.

Now, lay your bamboo mat flat and place a sheet of nori on top. Wet your hands to prevent sticking and spread a handful of seasoned sushi rice over the nori, leaving a 1-inch border at the top. Press the rice down with gentle but firm fingers.

Next, arrange a few strips of cucumber, carrot, avocado, and red bell pepper across the center of the rice. Add a leaf of butter lettuce for a refreshing crunch. Sprinkle some toasted sesame seeds over the vegetables for that extra nutty flavor.

It's rolling time! Lift the edge of the bamboo mat closest to you and start rolling away, tucking the fillings securely under the nori. Continue rolling, applying gentle pressure to keep everything tight and compact. Once you reach the end, seal the roll by moistening the top border of the nori with a bit of water.

With a sharp knife, cut the roll into bite-sized pieces, wiping the blade with a damp cloth between cuts to ensure clean slices. Arrange your vegetable rolls on a platter with a side of soy sauce, pickled ginger, and a dab of wasabi.

Feast your eyes and your taste buds on this garden-inspired roll! With every bite, feel the symphony of freshness and crunchiness. Remember, the true essence of sushi lies in the harmony of flavors. Happy rolling and even happier eating!

39. Futomaki Feast: Thick and Flavorful

Imagine a sushi roll so bountiful, it's a feast for the eyes and the palate. Each bite reveals a symphony of textures and flavors, a true celebration of culinary artistry. Prepare to be transported to a world where tradition meets innovation.

Preparation time: 45 minutes
Cooking time: 15 minutes
Ready-in time: 1 hour
Serving size: 4 people

Ingredients:
2 cups sushi rice
2 ½ cups water
¼ cup rice vinegar
2 tablespoons sugar
1 teaspoon salt
4 sheets nori (seaweed)
4 large eggs
1 tablespoon soy sauce
1 tablespoon mirin
1 cucumber, julienned
1 avocado, sliced
1 carrot, julienned
4 pieces kampyo (dried gourd), rehydrated
8 strips of unagi (grilled eel) or cooked shrimp
Pickled daikon radish, sliced into thin strips
Soy sauce for serving
Pickled ginger for serving
Wasabi for serving

Instructions:

To start, rinse the sushi rice under cold water until the water runs clear. This is key to achieving that perfect texture. Cook the rice with 2 ½ cups of water in a rice cooker. Once it's done, transfer it to a large bowl and let it cool slightly. In the meantime, mix the rice vinegar, sugar, and salt in a small bowl until dissolved. Gently fold this mixture into the cooked rice, ensuring each grain is well-coated. Let it cool to room temperature.

While the rice is cooling, let's prepare the tamago (Japanese omelet). Whisk together the eggs, soy sauce, and mirin. Heat a non-stick pan over medium heat, and pour a thin layer of the egg mixture into the pan. Cook until the bottom is set, then roll it to one side of the pan. Add another layer of egg and repeat the process until you have a layered omelet. Let it cool before slicing it into long strips.

Now, lay a sheet of nori, shiny side down, on a bamboo mat. With wet hands, spread a thin layer of sushi rice evenly over the nori, leaving a 1-inch border at the top. Arrange the fillings: cucumber, avocado, carrot, kampyo, unagi or shrimp, pickled daikon, and tamago in a line across the center of the rice.

Time to roll! Use the bamboo mat to roll the nori over the fillings, pressing gently but firmly to shape the roll. Continue rolling until you reach the border. Moisten the edge with a little water to seal the roll. Repeat with the remaining nori sheets and fillings.

Using a sharp knife, slice each roll into bite-sized pieces. Serve with soy sauce, pickled ginger, and a dab of wasabi. Savor each bite, and let the flavors dance on your tongue.

Ah, what a journey through flavors and textures! Remember, each roll is a story, and you've just crafted a masterpiece. Now, share this futomaki feast with friends and family, and watch as their eyes light up with delight. Until next time, keep rolling with passion!

40. Spider Roll: Soft Shell Crab Adventure

In the heart of the sushi world, the spider roll stands tall, a true delicacy that combines the crunch of soft shell crab with the elegance of sushi. Let's embark on this soft shell crab adventure together, shall we?

Preparation time: 30 minutes
Cooking time: 10 minutes
Ready-in time: 40 minutes
Serving size: 4 people

Ingredients:
2 soft shell crabs
1 cup tempura batter
1 cup cold water
1 cup all-purpose flour
Vegetable oil, for frying
4 sheets of nori (seaweed)
4 cups sushi rice, cooked and seasoned
1 cucumber, julienned
1 avocado, sliced
3 tablespoons unagi (eel) sauce
2 tablespoons sesame seeds
Pickled ginger, for garnish
Wasabi, for garnish
Soy sauce, for serving

Instructions:

Alright, my friends, let's start with the star of our show—the soft shell crab. First, mix the tempura batter: combine the tempura batter mix with cold water in a bowl. You want it to be cold, as this will give our crab that perfect, crispy texture.

Next, pat the crabs dry and dredge them lightly in flour. This will help the batter stick. Dip each crab into the tempura batter, ensuring they're well-coated. Heat the vegetable oil in a deep frying pan or pot until it reaches about 350°F (175°C). Carefully place the crabs into the hot oil and fry until golden and crispy, about 3-4 minutes. Once done, let them drain on a paper towel-lined plate.

Now, the fun part begins. Place a sheet of nori on your bamboo sushi mat, shiny side down. Wet your hands slightly to handle the sushi rice without it sticking. Spread a thin layer of sushi rice evenly over the nori, leaving an inch at the top edge. Sprinkle some sesame seeds over the rice for an extra crunch.

Turn the nori and rice over so the rice is facing down. Lay a few pieces of cucumber and avocado along the middle of the nori. Place the fried soft shell crab on top of the vegetables. Now, roll it up tightly, using the bamboo mat to help shape it. Apply gentle pressure to ensure it holds together.

To finish, slice the roll into bite-sized pieces with a sharp knife. Drizzle unagi sauce over the top for that beautiful glaze and extra flavor. Serve with pickled ginger, wasabi, and soy sauce on the side.

"Bravo! You've created a masterpiece worthy of any sushi bar. Remember, every roll tells a story, and yours just captured the essence of the sea. Until our next culinary adventure, keep rolling with passion and precision!"

41. Nakamoto's Roll: A Culinary Masterpiece

In the heart of culinary artistry, the true essence of sushi unfolds in delicate flavors and meticulous craftsmanship. Let's embark on a journey where tradition meets innovation, creating a symphony of taste in every bite.

Preparation time: 30 minutes
Cooking time: 10 minutes
Ready-in time: 40 minutes
Serving size: 4 people

Ingredients:
2 cups sushi rice
2 1/4 cups water
1/4 cup rice vinegar
2 tablespoons sugar
1 teaspoon salt
4 sheets nori (seaweed)
8 ounces fresh tuna, thinly sliced
8 ounces fresh salmon, thinly sliced
1 avocado, thinly sliced
1 cucumber, julienned
2 tablespoons tobiko (flying fish roe)
Soy sauce, for serving
Pickled ginger, for serving
Wasabi, for serving

Instructions:

Alright, let's dive into creating this masterpiece. First, we need to prepare our sushi rice. Rinse the sushi rice under cold water until the water runs clear. Combine the rinsed rice and water in a rice cooker and let it cook. Once it's done, transfer it to a large bowl and let it cool for a few minutes.

Now, in a small saucepan, gently heat the rice vinegar, sugar, and salt until the sugar dissolves. Pour this mixture over the cooled rice and fold it in carefully to avoid mashing the grains. Our seasoned rice is now ready.

Next, lay out your bamboo mat and place a sheet of nori on top, shiny side down. Wet your hands to prevent sticking, and take a handful of sushi rice, spreading it evenly over the nori, leaving about an inch at the top edge.

Now comes the fun part. Layer the slices of tuna and salmon horizontally across the center of the rice. Add a few slices of avocado and a sprinkle of cucumber for that refreshing crunch. Carefully roll the sushi away from you, using the bamboo mat to help shape it into a tight cylinder.

Once rolled, sprinkle a bit of tobiko on top for a burst of color and flavor. Repeat the process with the remaining ingredients.

Slice each roll into bite-sized pieces, and arrange them artfully on a platter. Serve with soy sauce, pickled ginger, and wasabi on the side.

"There you have it, a creation that captures the spirit and elegance of sushi making. Enjoy this culinary journey, and may each bite bring you closer to sushi mastery!"

42. Volcano Roll: Spicy Eruption

Imagine the sudden, thrilling burst of a volcano right on your plate. This roll is not just about heat, it's an explosion of flavors that will take your taste buds on an unforgettable adventure.

Preparation time: 30 minutes
Cooking time: 10 minutes
Ready-in time: 40 minutes
Serving size: 4 people

Ingredients:
2 cups sushi rice, cooked and seasoned
4 sheets nori (seaweed)
1 avocado, sliced
1 cucumber, julienned
8 pieces imitation crab sticks
1/2 cup spicy mayo
1/4 cup eel sauce
1/2 cup tempura flakes
1/2 pound scallops, diced
1 tablespoon sriracha
1 tablespoon sesame oil
1 tablespoon soy sauce
1 green onion, finely chopped
1 tablespoon tobiko (flying fish roe)

Instructions:

Alright, let's get rolling! First, lay out your bamboo mat and cover it with plastic wrap. Place a sheet of nori on the mat, shiny side down. Wet your hands to keep the rice from sticking, then spread an even layer of sushi rice over the nori, leaving about an inch at the top edge.

Flip the nori over so that the rice is now facing down. Arrange a few slices of avocado, cucumber, and two crab sticks horizontally across the middle. Carefully roll the nori over the filling, using the bamboo mat to help shape it into a tight cylinder. Press firmly to seal the edge. Repeat this process for all four rolls.

Now comes the fun part - the eruption! In a small bowl, mix the diced scallops with sriracha, sesame oil, and soy sauce. Spoon this spicy mixture generously over the top of each roll. Drizzle with spicy mayo and eel sauce. Sprinkle tempura flakes over the top for an extra crunch.

Finish with a flourish of green onions and tobiko. To serve, slice each roll into bite-sized pieces, about six to eight per roll.

"Ah, the symphony of flavors and textures! I hope your taste buds are dancing. Remember, sushi making is an art form, and you've just mastered a fiery masterpiece. Until next time, keep rolling with passion!"

43. Lobster Tempura Roll: Luxurious Indulgence

Imagine the thrill of biting into a roll that combines the delicate sweetness of lobster with the crisp lightness of tempura. This dish is not just food; it's an experience that whispers the secrets of the ocean.

Preparation time: 20 minutes
Cooking time: 15 minutes
Ready-in time: 35 minutes
Serving size: 4 people

Ingredients:
1 live lobster
1 cup tempura batter mix
1 cup cold water
1 cup sushi rice
2 sheets nori (seaweed)
1 cucumber, julienned
1 avocado, sliced
1 tablespoon tobiko (flying fish roe)
Soy sauce, for dipping
Vegetable oil, for frying

Instructions:

First, let's prepare our lobster. We want the sweetest, freshest meat, so bring a pot of water to a boil and gently place the lobster in, cooking it for about 8 minutes until it's vibrant red. Once cooked, extract that luscious meat, and if you can, try to keep the claws intact for a stunning presentation.

Now, mix up your tempura batter. The key here is cold water; it gives that iconic light and airy crunch. Combine the tempura batter mix with the cold water and stir just until combined. It's okay if it's a little lumpy.

Heat your vegetable oil in a deep pot until it reaches 350°F (175°C). Dip the lobster chunks into the batter, then gently lay them into the hot oil. Fry until golden and crispy, about 2-3 minutes. Let them rest on a paper towel to drain any excess oil.

With the lobster resting, it's time to prepare your sushi rice. Spread a thin, even layer of rice onto a sheet of nori. Remember, a wet fingertip helps prevent sticking. Lay your julienned cucumber and avocado slices across the center, and then nestle in those beautiful lobster tempura pieces.

Carefully roll your sushi using a bamboo mat, squeezing gently but firmly to create a tight roll. Just before you finish, sprinkle a touch of tobiko across the top for that extra burst of flavor and color.

Slice your roll into eight even pieces with a sharp, wet knife. Serve with a side of soy sauce for dipping, and get ready to indulge in luxury.

Every bite of this Lobster Tempura Roll is a symphony of textures and flavors that transports you to a seaside paradise. Share it with friends and family and watch their eyes light up with each delicious mouthful. Enjoy your culinary journey!

44. Mango Tango Roll: Sweet and Savory

The dance of flavors in this sushi roll will make your taste buds sway to a tropical rhythm. Imagine the sweetness of ripe mango mingling with the savory essence of crab and the slight kick of spicy mayo. Let's get rolling!

Preparation time: 20 minutes
Cooking time: 20 minutes
Ready-in time: 40 minutes
Serving size: 4 people

Ingredients:
2 cups sushi rice, cooked and seasoned
4 sheets nori (seaweed)
1 ripe mango, thinly sliced
200 grams imitation crab meat, shredded
1 avocado, thinly sliced
2 tablespoons spicy mayo
1 cucumber, julienned
1 teaspoon sesame seeds
Soy sauce, for dipping
Pickled ginger, for serving
Wasabi, for serving

Instructions:

Alright, let's begin this flavorful adventure! First, lay down your bamboo sushi mat and cover it with plastic wrap to keep things tidy. Place a sheet of nori, shiny side down, on the mat. With wet fingers, spread about half a cup of sushi rice evenly over the nori. Be gentle, like you're caressing a delicate piece of art.

Now, it's time to flip the nori so the rice is facing down. Don't worry, it's easier than it sounds! Arrange a few slices of mango, crab meat, avocado, and cucumber in a neat line across the nori, about an inch from the bottom edge.

Here's where we can add a little zing! Drizzle a bit of that spicy mayo over the fillings. Now, using the bamboo mat, start rolling from the bottom, applying gentle pressure to keep everything tight and together. Continue rolling until you reach the top edge of the nori.

Once your roll is complete, let's give it a little garnish. Sprinkle sesame seeds over the top of the roll for that extra crunch and nutty flavor. With a sharp knife, slice the roll into bite-sized pieces. Remember, a clean knife makes clean cuts, so wipe it with a damp cloth between slices.

Arrange your Mango Tango Rolls on a plate. Serve with soy sauce, pickled ginger, and wasabi on the side.

Bravo! You've just crafted a symphony of flavors that will transport you to a tropical paradise. Enjoy the dance of sweet and savory with every bite. Until our next culinary adventure, keep your knives sharp and your spirit sharper!

45. Zen Garden Roll: Cucumber and Avocado Bliss

In the heart of simplicity lies beauty, and in the essence of nature, we find balance. This roll captures the serenity of a Zen garden, bringing a harmonious blend of cucumber and avocado that dances gently on your palate.

Preparation time: 20 minutes
Cooking time: 20 minutes
Ready-in time: 40 minutes
Serving size: 4 people

Ingredients:
2 cups sushi rice
2 1/2 cups water
1/4 cup rice vinegar
2 tablespoons sugar
1 teaspoon salt
4 sheets of nori (seaweed)
1 cucumber, julienned
2 avocados, sliced
1 tablespoon toasted sesame seeds
Soy sauce, for serving
Pickled ginger, for serving
Wasabi, for serving

Instructions:

Let's begin by preparing our sushi rice, the foundation of all great rolls. Rinse the sushi rice under cold water until the water runs clear. This step is crucial to remove excess starch. Combine the rice and water in a rice cooker and let it do its magic. Once cooked, transfer the rice to a large bowl and let it cool slightly.

While the rice is still warm, mix together rice vinegar, sugar, and salt until dissolved. Pour this mixture over the rice, gently folding it in with a wooden spoon. Try not to mash the grains; we want them to remain whole and fluffy.

Now, let's assemble the Zen Garden Roll. Place a sheet of nori on a bamboo sushi mat, shiny side down. Wet your hands to prevent sticking and spread a thin, even layer of sushi rice over the nori, leaving about an inch at the top edge.

Sprinkle a few toasted sesame seeds over the rice for a subtle crunch. Lay down a line of julienned cucumber and avocado slices horizontally across the center of the rice. The crispness of the cucumber and the creamy richness of the avocado create a beautiful contrast.

Using the bamboo mat, carefully roll the nori over the filling, pressing gently but firmly to shape the roll. Once you reach the exposed edge of the nori, wet it slightly to seal the roll.

With a sharp knife, cut the roll into eight even pieces. To keep the knife from sticking, dip it in water between cuts. Arrange the pieces on a platter, and serve with soy sauce, pickled ginger, and a dab of wasabi.

Just as the Zen garden brings tranquility to the mind, this roll brings harmony to the senses. May each bite transport you to a place of peaceful bliss. Until our next culinary adventure, may your kitchen be filled with joy and creativity!

46. Sumo Roll: Big and Bold

Imagine a sumo wrestler, standing tall and proud, ready to take on the world with strength and grace. That's what this roll embodies—bold flavors, hearty ingredients, and a presence that commands attention. Are you ready to roll with the big leagues?

Preparation time: 30 minutes
Cooking time: 10 minutes
Ready-in time: 40 minutes
Serving size: 4 people

Ingredients:
2 cups sushi rice, cooked and seasoned
4 sheets nori (seaweed)
1 avocado, thinly sliced
1 cucumber, julienned
1 carrot, julienned
8 pieces shrimp tempura
4 oz crab meat
2 tbsp mayonnaise
2 tbsp sriracha
1 tbsp soy sauce
1 tbsp rice vinegar
1 tsp sesame oil
Sesame seeds for garnish
Pickled ginger and wasabi for serving

Instructions:

First, let's get that sushi rice ready. If you haven't cooked it yet, make sure it's done and seasoned with rice vinegar. Now, lay out your bamboo mat and place a sheet of plastic wrap over it. Trust me, it makes the rolling easier and less sticky. Place a sheet of nori on the mat, shiny side down.

Wet your hands to prevent sticking and spread about half a cup of sushi rice evenly over the nori, leaving a small border at the top. Flip the nori over so the rice side is down—yes, we're going inside-out style today.

Now, it's time for the stars of the show! Lay down two pieces of shrimp tempura in the center, followed by a few slices of avocado, cucumber, and carrot. Add some crab meat for that extra oomph.

In a small bowl, mix the mayonnaise, sriracha, soy sauce, and sesame oil. Drizzle this spicy concoction over the ingredients in the center. Feeling bold? Add a bit more!

Using the bamboo mat, carefully roll the nori over the filling, tucking it in tightly. Keep rolling until you reach the border, then give it a gentle squeeze to shape it into a firm roll. Repeat for the other three sheets of nori.

Once all your rolls are complete, slice them into bite-sized pieces with a sharp, wet knife. Sprinkle sesame seeds over the top for that final touch.

Serve your Sumo Rolls with pickled ginger and wasabi on the side. Enjoy the big, bold flavors!

Sumo Roll champions, you have created a masterpiece! These rolls are not just food; they are an experience—like a sumo match in your mouth. May your culinary journey continue with the same strength and flavor! Until next time, happy rolling!

47. Cherry Blossom Roll: A Touch of Elegance

Imagine the ephemeral beauty of cherry blossoms captured in a sushi roll. This dish isn't just food—it's an ode to the fleeting beauty of nature, an expression of elegance wrapped in seaweed and rice.

Preparation time: 30 minutes
Cooking time: 20 minutes
Ready-in time: 50 minutes
Serving size: 4 people

Ingredients:
2 cups sushi rice
2 1/2 cups water
1/4 cup rice vinegar
2 tablespoons sugar
1 teaspoon salt
4 sheets nori (seaweed)
8 ounces fresh tuna, thinly sliced
1 small cucumber, julienned
1 avocado, thinly sliced
2 tablespoons pickled ginger, finely chopped
2 tablespoons wasabi
1 tablespoon sesame seeds
Soy sauce for serving
Pink pickled radish for garnish

Instructions:

Alright, let's begin this culinary journey. First, let's cook our sushi rice. Rinse the rice thoroughly under cold water until the water runs clear. Combine the rice and water in a rice cooker and let it do its magic. Once cooked, transfer the rice to a large bowl and let it cool slightly.

While the rice is still warm, mix in the rice vinegar, sugar, and salt. Use a wooden paddle or spoon to gently fold the seasoning into the rice. Be careful not to mash the grains; we want them to stay intact and beautiful.

Now, let's roll—literally! Place a sheet of nori, shiny side down, on a bamboo sushi mat. Wet your hands with a bit of water to prevent sticking and spread a thin layer of sushi rice over the nori, leaving about an inch at the top edge.

In the center of the rice, lay a line of thinly sliced tuna, cucumber, avocado, and a sprinkle of finely chopped pickled ginger. Add a dash of wasabi if you're feeling adventurous.

Lift the bamboo mat edge closest to you and begin to roll the sushi away from you, applying gentle but firm pressure. Keep rolling until you reach the edge, then give it a final press to seal.

Using a sharp knife dipped in water, slice the roll into six or eight pieces. Arrange the sushi pieces on a platter and garnish with sesame seeds and pink pickled radish slices for that cherry blossom effect.

Serve with soy sauce and an extra dollop of wasabi on the side. And there you have it—a touch of elegance on your plate.

Ah, the Cherry Blossom Roll! A dish that whispers the poetry of spring with every bite. May your culinary adventures be as delightful and ephemeral as sakura in bloom. Until next time, savor the art of sushi—one roll at a time!

48. Firecracker Roll: Explosive Flavor

When I think of this roll, I imagine a symphony of flavors, each bite an explosion, a celebration of taste and texture. This is no ordinary roll; it's a firecracker of culinary delight, promising excitement with every bite.

Preparation time: 30 minutes
Cooking time: 10 minutes
Ready-in time: 40 minutes
Serving size: 4 people

Ingredients:
2 cups sushi rice
2 1/2 cups water
1/4 cup rice vinegar
2 tablespoons sugar
1 teaspoon salt
8 sheets nori (seaweed)
1 cucumber, julienned
1 avocado, sliced
8 ounces spicy tuna (sashimi-grade tuna mixed with sriracha and mayo)
8 pieces shrimp tempura
1/4 cup tobiko (flying fish roe)
2 tablespoons sriracha sauce
2 tablespoons Japanese mayo
1/4 cup tempura flakes
Soy sauce, for serving
Pickled ginger, for serving
Wasabi, for serving

Instructions:

First things first, let's prepare our sushi rice. Rinse the rice under cold water until it runs clear, then combine it with water in a rice cooker. Once cooked, let it steam for an additional 10 minutes. In a small saucepan, gently heat the rice vinegar, sugar, and salt until dissolved. Fold this mixture into your warm rice and let it cool to room temperature.

Lay out a bamboo sushi mat and place a sheet of nori on top, shiny side down. Wet your hands to prevent sticking and spread a thin layer of sushi rice over the nori, leaving a small margin at the top. Now, flip the nori sheet so the rice is facing down on the mat.

For the filling, lay a strip of cucumber, avocado slices, a generous spoonful of spicy tuna, and two pieces of shrimp tempura horizontally across the center of the nori. Carefully roll the sushi mat away from you, applying even pressure to form a tight roll. Repeat with remaining ingredients.

Now, for the topping that will make your Firecracker Roll truly explosive. Mix the sriracha sauce with Japanese mayo, then drizzle generously over each roll. Sprinkle with tobiko and tempura flakes for that crunch.

Slice each roll into bite-sized pieces, arranging them artfully on a platter. Serve with soy sauce, pickled ginger, and wasabi on the side.

Prepare yourself for a taste sensation that dances on the palate and leaves a lingering spark. Every roll is an adventure, an invitation to savor the intricate layers of flavor. Enjoy the journey, and may your culinary creations always ignite joy.

49. Ocean's Bounty Roll: A Seafood Medley

Embark on a journey to the deep blue with this vibrant roll, where the flavors of the ocean come alive in every bite. This roll celebrates the harmonious dance of textures and tastes, a true testament to the bounty of the sea.

Preparation time: 30 minutes
Cooking time: 10 minutes
Ready-in time: 40 minutes
Serving size: 4 people

Ingredients:
1 cup sushi rice, cooked and seasoned
4 sheets nori (seaweed)
4 oz fresh tuna, thinly sliced
4 oz fresh salmon, thinly sliced
4 oz cooked shrimp, chopped
1 avocado, thinly sliced
1 cucumber, julienned
2 tbsp tobiko (flying fish roe)
2 tbsp Japanese mayonnaise
1 tbsp soy sauce
1 tsp wasabi
Pickled ginger, for serving
Soy sauce, for serving

Instructions:

Alright, sushi enthusiasts, let's dive into the ocean's bounty! Begin with your sushi rice – it should be perfectly seasoned and just cool enough to handle. Lay out your bamboo mat and place a sheet of nori on top. Spread a thin layer of sushi rice evenly over the nori, leaving a small border at the top.

Next, let's layer the treasures of the sea. Start with a few slices of fresh tuna and salmon, laying them horizontally across the center of the rice. Add a generous portion of chopped shrimp, a few slices of creamy avocado, and the crisp cucumber strips.

Now, gently lift the bamboo mat, guiding the roll into shape. Roll it tightly but gently, ensuring the filling stays snug inside. Seal the edge with a touch of water.

Here comes the fun part – the topping! Spread a thin layer of Japanese mayonnaise over the roll and sprinkle with vibrant tobiko for that pop of color and crunch. If you like a bit of heat, mix a dab of wasabi into your soy sauce for dipping.

Slice your roll into bite-sized pieces, arrange them beautifully on a plate, and serve with pickled ginger and extra soy sauce on the side.

"Ah, you've done it! You've captured the essence of the ocean in a single roll. Savor each bite, let the flavors wash over you, and remember, the sea is always full of surprises. Until next time, keep rolling and exploring!"

50. Yuzu Citrus Roll: Refreshing Zest

In the heart of summer, when the sun dances on the horizon and the air is filled with a zest for life, nothing captures the essence of freshness like the tangy embrace of yuzu. Prepare to be invigorated with each bite of this delightful Yuzu Citrus Roll.

Preparation time: 25 minutes
Cooking time: 10 minutes
Ready-in time: 35 minutes
Serving size: 4 people

Ingredients:
2 cups sushi rice
2 1/2 cups water
1/4 cup rice vinegar
2 tablespoons sugar
1 teaspoon salt
1 yuzu, juiced and zested
1/2 cucumber, julienned
1 avocado, sliced
4 sheets nori (seaweed)
8 ounces fresh tuna, thinly sliced
1 tablespoon sesame seeds
Soy sauce, for serving
Pickled ginger, for serving

Instructions:

First, let's bring our sushi rice to life. Rinse the rice under cold water until the water runs clear. Combine the rice and water in a rice cooker and let it steam to perfection. Meanwhile, in a small saucepan, gently heat the rice vinegar, sugar, and salt until dissolved. Once your rice is ready, fold in the seasoned vinegar mixture while fanning the rice to cool it down. This will give your rice that perfect glossy texture.

Now, let's get citrusy! Juice and zest your yuzu, and set it aside. Its bright, aromatic notes will elevate your roll to new heights.

Lay out your bamboo mat and place a sheet of nori on top. Dampen your hands with water to prevent sticking, and spread an even layer of sushi rice over the nori, leaving a small border at the top. Sprinkle the yuzu juice and zest over the rice, adding an invigorating burst of flavor.

Layer the cucumber julienne, avocado slices, and fresh tuna along the center of the rice. Carefully lift the bamboo mat and roll it tightly, tucking the ingredients snugly inside. Keep rolling until you reach the border, then dab a little water on the edge of the nori to seal the roll.

Using a sharp knife, slice the roll into bite-sized pieces. Arrange them beautifully on a plate, sprinkle with sesame seeds, and serve alongside soy sauce and pickled ginger.

"Allow the exhilarating flavors of yuzu and fresh tuna to dance on your palate, a symphony of tastes that will transport you to the vibrant streets of Tokyo. Enjoy every refreshing bite and let it remind you of the joy found in culinary artistry!"

51. Avocado Nigiri: Creamy Simplicity

In the world of sushi, simplicity often holds profound elegance. Here, we transform the humble avocado into a luxurious bite, celebrating its buttery texture and delicate flavor. Let's embark on a journey where minimalism meets mastery.

Preparation time: 20 minutes
Cooking time: 10 minutes
Ready-in time: 30 minutes
Serving size: 4 people

Ingredients:
2 cups sushi rice
2 1/2 cups water
1/4 cup rice vinegar
2 tablespoons sugar
1 teaspoon salt
2 ripe avocados
1 lemon
Soy sauce for serving
Wasabi for serving

Instructions:

First, let's set the foundation with perfectly seasoned sushi rice. Rinse the sushi rice under cold water until the water runs clear. This is crucial for achieving that perfect sticky texture. Combine the rice and water in a rice cooker and let it cook. If you don't have a rice cooker, no worries! You can cook the rice in a pot by bringing it to a boil, then reducing the heat to low and covering it until all the water is absorbed, which should take about 15 minutes. Once cooked, let it sit for another 10 minutes off the heat.

While the rice is cooking, let's prepare the seasoning. In a small saucepan over low heat, combine the rice vinegar, sugar, and salt until the sugar dissolves completely. Pour this mixture over your cooked rice and gently fold it in. Be careful not to smash the rice; we want each grain to stay intact. Allow the rice to cool to room temperature.

Now, onto our star ingredient: the avocado. Cut the avocados in half, remove the pit, and carefully peel off the skin. Slice each half into thin, even slices. To prevent browning, drizzle a little lemon juice over the slices.

Time to assemble! Wet your hands with a bit of water to prevent the rice from sticking. Take a small amount of rice and shape it into an oval mound, about two fingers wide and one finger high. Gently press an avocado slice onto each mound of rice, letting its creamy texture embrace the seasoned grains.

Arrange your avocado nigiri on a beautiful platter. Serve with soy sauce and a dab of wasabi on the side. Each bite is a testament to the beauty of simplicity and the harmony of flavors.

"Bravo! You've crafted a masterpiece that embodies the essence of sushi simplicity. Remember, it's the love and care you infuse into each step that makes every bite magical. Relish this creation, and let each mouthful transport you to the serene landscapes of Japan."

52. Cucumber Maki: Refreshing Crunch

Imagine a warm summer day, the sun caressing your face, and a cool breeze whispering through the leaves. That's the essence we capture with our Cucumber Maki: a symphony of refreshing crunch in every bite. Let's roll!

Preparation time: 20 minutes
Cooking time: 20 minutes
Ready-in time: 40 minutes
Serving size: 4 people

Ingredients:
2 cups sushi rice, cooked and seasoned
4 sheets nori (seaweed)
1 cucumber, julienned
1 avocado, sliced thinly
2 tablespoons rice vinegar
1 tablespoon sugar
1 teaspoon salt
Soy sauce for serving
Pickled ginger for serving
Wasabi for serving

Instructions:

Alright, let's embark on this culinary journey together. First, we'll prepare the star of the show: sushi rice. Once you've cooked your rice to perfection, mix in the rice vinegar, sugar, and salt. This will give our rice that sushi tang. Let it cool to room temperature.

Now, grab a bamboo sushi mat and place a sheet of nori on top, shiny side down. Wet your hands with a little water to prevent sticking and spread a thin, even layer of sushi rice over the nori, leaving about an inch at the top edge. This will help seal our roll later.

Next, arrange the julienned cucumber and avocado slices horizontally across the center of the rice. These two ingredients are like a refreshing duet, harmonizing perfectly with each bite.

Time to roll! Lift the edge of the bamboo mat closest to you and begin to roll away, keeping the ingredients snugly inside. Go slowly, applying gentle pressure to keep everything tight and compact. When you reach the end, wet the exposed edge of the nori with a little water and press to seal.

Using a sharp knife, slice the roll into bite-sized pieces. Remember, a clean knife will give you those beautiful, precise cuts, so wipe it between slices.

Serve your Cucumber Maki with soy sauce, pickled ginger, and a dab of wasabi. The crunch of the cucumber, the creaminess of the avocado, and the tangy rice will dance on your palate.

"Congratulations, you've just crafted a masterpiece of simplicity and flavor. Enjoy this refreshing crunch and let it transport you to a zen-like state. Keep rolling, and may your sushi adventures be ever delightful!"

53. Pickled Radish Roll: Tart and Tangy

A dish that sings with the bright notes of pickled radish, this roll is a symphony of tart and tangy flavors, harmonized with the delicate balance of rice and nori. Let's embark on this culinary journey together, shall we?

Preparation time: 30 minutes
Cooking time: 20 minutes
Ready-in time: 50 minutes
Serving size: 4 people

Ingredients:
2 cups sushi rice
2 1/4 cups water
1/4 cup rice vinegar
2 tablespoons sugar
1 teaspoon salt
8 sheets nori (seaweed)
1 cup pickled radish, julienned
1 avocado, sliced thinly
1 cucumber, julienned
Soy sauce, for serving
Pickled ginger, for serving
Wasabi, for serving

Instructions:

First, my friends, we start with the sushi rice. Rinse the rice under cold water until the water runs clear. This is crucial for that perfect, sticky consistency. Combine the rinsed rice and water in a rice cooker and let it work its magic. Once done, transfer the rice to a large bowl and let it cool slightly.

While the rice is still warm, mix in the rice vinegar, sugar, and salt. Gently fold the mixture into the rice. This step is where the rice takes on its flavor, so be sure to do it with care and love.

Now, let's assemble our rolls! Place a sheet of nori on a bamboo sushi mat, shiny side down. Wet your hands to prevent sticking and spread a thin layer of rice over the nori, leaving about an inch at the top edge.

Next, lay out the julienned pickled radish, avocado slices, and cucumber strips horizontally across the center of the rice. These ingredients will provide that delightful tart and tangy punch we're aiming for.

Time to roll! Using the bamboo mat, lift the edge of the nori closest to you and begin rolling away from you, applying gentle pressure to keep the roll tight. Moisten the top edge of the nori with a bit of water to seal the roll.

Once rolled, use a sharp knife to cut the roll into eight even pieces. Remember, a sharp knife is key to clean cuts! Repeat the process with the remaining ingredients.

Serve your pickled radish rolls with soy sauce, pickled ginger, and a dab of wasabi on the side. Enjoy the burst of flavors in every bite.

"Ah, the joy of creating such a vibrant and zesty dish! May your rolls always be tight and your flavors always balanced. Until next time, keep rolling and savoring each moment!"

54. Tofu Pockets: Inari Sushi Sweetness

The first time I tasted inari sushi, I was taken aback by its delicate balance of sweetness and umami. Who knew such simple ingredients could create a symphony on the palate? Now, let's recreate that magic in your kitchen!

Preparation time: 20 minutes
Cooking time: 20 minutes
Ready-in time: 40 minutes
Serving size: 4 people

Ingredients:
2 cups sushi rice
2 ½ cups water
¼ cup rice vinegar
2 tablespoons sugar
1 teaspoon salt
1 package aburaage (fried tofu pockets)
½ cup soy sauce
½ cup mirin
2 tablespoons sugar
½ teaspoon dashi powder
1 tablespoon sesame seeds
1 small cucumber, julienned
1 small carrot, julienned
Pickled ginger, for garnish

Instructions:

Alright, let's dive in! Start by rinsing the sushi rice until the water runs clear. This helps remove excess starch, making the rice perfectly sticky. Add the rinsed rice and water to a rice cooker and let it do its magic. If you don't have a rice cooker, a covered pot on the stove works just fine.

While the rice is cooking, let's prepare the tofu pockets. In a small saucepan, combine soy sauce, mirin, sugar, and dashi powder. Bring the mixture to a gentle boil and then reduce to a simmer. Carefully add the tofu pockets and let them soak up all that flavorful goodness for about 10 minutes. Turn off the heat and let them cool.

Now, the sushi rice should be done. Transfer it to a large bowl and gently fold in the rice vinegar, sugar, and salt until well combined. Allow the rice to cool to room temperature.

Time to fill those pockets! Gently open each tofu pocket and stuff it with the seasoned sushi rice. Don't overfill—just enough to create a lovely, plump shape. Sprinkle a few sesame seeds over each pocket for a bit of crunch and visual appeal.

For some added color and texture, garnish each tofu pocket with julienned cucumber and carrot. A little pickled ginger on the side adds a nice zing!

And there you have it—Tofu Pockets: Inari Sushi Sweetness ready to be enjoyed.

Cooking is like painting a canvas, where each ingredient adds a stroke of flavor, transforming a simple dish into a masterpiece. Enjoy every bite and let the symphony of tastes serenade your senses!

55. Asparagus Tempura Roll: Delightful Crisp

Imagine a symphony of textures and flavors, where the orchestra of crisp asparagus tempura plays in perfect harmony with creamy avocado and delicate sushi rice. Let's embark on this culinary journey together, crafting an asparagus tempura roll that's not just food, but an experience.

Preparation time: 20 minutes
Cooking time: 10 minutes
Ready-in time: 30 minutes
Serving size: 4 people

Ingredients:
Sushi rice - 2 cups, cooked and seasoned
Nori sheets - 4
Fresh asparagus - 8 spears, trimmed
Tempura batter mix - 1 cup
Ice-cold water - 3/4 cup
All-purpose flour - 1/4 cup
Vegetable oil - for frying
Avocado - 1, sliced thinly
Soy sauce - for serving
Pickled ginger - for serving
Wasabi - for serving

Instructions:

First, prepare your workspace and gather all your ingredients. Sushi making is an art, and like all art, it starts with the right tools and materials. Cook your sushi rice according to your favorite method, and let it cool to room temperature.

While the rice cools, let's move on to our star – the asparagus. Trim those vibrant green spears and get them ready for their crispy transformation. Mix the tempura batter by combining the tempura mix with ice-cold water. Remember, the colder the better; it's the secret to that perfect crunch.

Heat your vegetable oil in a deep pan to 350°F (175°C). Lightly coat the asparagus spears in flour before dipping them into the tempura batter. Fry them until golden brown and irresistibly crispy, which should take about 2-3 minutes. Let them drain on a paper towel to keep that crunch intact.

Now, it's time to roll. Place a nori sheet, shiny side down, on your bamboo mat. Wet your hands to prevent sticking and spread a thin, even layer of sushi rice over the nori, leaving a small border at the top. Lay two tempura asparagus spears and a few slices of avocado onto the rice.

Carefully roll the sushi, using the bamboo mat to help shape it tightly. Moisten the edge of the nori to seal the roll. Repeat the process with the remaining ingredients.

Slice each roll into 8 pieces using a sharp knife. Serve with soy sauce, pickled ginger, and a dab of wasabi.

Your journey through the flavors of Japan doesn't end here. Each bite of this Asparagus Tempura Roll promises a new adventure on your palate. Keep exploring, keep creating, and remember, the heart of sushi lies in the joy of sharing it. Until next time, keep your knives sharp and your spirits high!

56. Carrot Ginger Roll: Earthy and Fresh

Ever thought of capturing the essence of a vibrant garden in a sushi roll? With the crispness of fresh carrots and the zing of ginger, this roll invites you to experience flavors that dance on your tongue. Let's embark on this delicious journey together!

Preparation time: 25 minutes
Cooking time: 15 minutes
Ready-in time: 40 minutes
Serving size: 4 people

Ingredients:
1 cup sushi rice
1 1/4 cups water
2 tablespoons rice vinegar
1 tablespoon sugar
1 teaspoon salt
2 medium carrots, julienned
1 tablespoon fresh ginger, grated
4 sheets nori
1 avocado, sliced
1 cucumber, julienned
Soy sauce for serving
Pickled ginger for serving

Instructions:

First, let's get that sushi rice perfect. Rinse the sushi rice under cold water until the water runs clear. Combine the rice and water in a medium saucepan and bring it to a boil. Once boiling, reduce the heat to low, cover, and simmer for about 15 minutes. Then, remove it from the heat and let it sit with the lid on for another 10 minutes.

While the rice is cooking, let's prepare the seasoning. In a small bowl, mix the rice vinegar, sugar, and salt until everything is dissolved. Once the rice is ready, fold in the vinegar mixture and let it cool to room temperature.

Now, onto the stars of our roll – the carrots and ginger. Julienne the carrots finely, and grate the fresh ginger. The combination of these two will bring a refreshing punch to the roll.

Lay out a bamboo sushi mat and place a sheet of nori on top. Wet your hands to prevent sticking and spread a thin layer of rice over the nori, leaving about an inch at the top edge. Arrange the julienned carrots, grated ginger, avocado slices, and cucumber strips along the bottom edge of the rice.

Time to roll! Using the bamboo mat, roll the nori tightly over the fillings, pressing firmly as you go. Moisten the top edge with a little water to seal the roll. Repeat this process with the remaining ingredients.

With a sharp knife, slice each roll into bite-sized pieces. Serve your Carrot Ginger Rolls with soy sauce and pickled ginger on the side.

Cooking is an adventure, and today, we've traveled to a garden bursting with flavor! Enjoy every bite of your Carrot Ginger Roll. Remember, the essence of a great dish is the love and passion you put into it. Happy rolling, my friends!

57. Spinach Gomae Maki: Nutty Delight

Picture this: a delicate roll of velvety spinach, perfectly seasoned with a robust sesame sauce, wrapped up in a blanket of tender nori. This journey of flavors is both an homage to simplicity and a celebration of nature's bounty.

Preparation time: 20 minutes
Cooking time: 2 minutes
Ready-in time: 22 minutes
Serving size: 4 people

Ingredients:
8 cups fresh spinach leaves
4 sheets of nori
1 cup cooked sushi rice
2 tablespoons sesame seeds, toasted
2 tablespoons soy sauce
2 tablespoons mirin
2 tablespoons sugar
1 tablespoon rice vinegar
1 teaspoon sesame oil

Instructions:

Alright, let's get started! First, bring a pot of water to a boil and blanch the spinach for about 1-2 minutes, just until it wilts. Quickly drain and plunge it into ice water to stop the cooking. Squeeze out the excess water and set the spinach aside.

Now, for the sesame sauce, we combine our toasted sesame seeds, soy sauce, mirin, sugar, rice vinegar, and sesame oil in a bowl. Mix this well until the sugar dissolves and everything comes together in a harmonious, nutty blend.

On a clean surface, lay down a sheet of nori and spread a thin layer of sushi rice over it, leaving about an inch at the top edge free. Wet your hands to prevent sticking if needed!

Next, arrange a portion of the blanched spinach in a line across the middle of the rice. Drizzle a generous amount of our sesame sauce over the spinach, allowing it to seep into the leaves, imbuing them with that rich, nutty flavor.

Now, carefully roll the nori over the spinach, using your fingers to press and shape it into a tight roll. Moisten the top edge of the nori with a bit of water to seal the roll.

Repeat this process with the remaining nori sheets, rice, and spinach. Once all the rolls are made, use a sharp knife to slice them into bite-sized pieces, wiping the blade between cuts for clean edges.

And there you have it – Spinach Gomae Maki, a nutty delight ready to be savored!

Rolling sushi is like crafting a beautiful story – each ingredient adds its own chapter, and together they create a masterpiece. Enjoy every bite of this nutty delight, and let it remind you that the simplest ingredients often make the most unforgettable dishes.

58. Sweet Potato Roll: Comforting Layers

In the world of sushi, there are flavors that dance and textures that sing. This Sweet Potato Roll is a melody of comfort and elegance, a true homage to the balance of simplicity and sophistication.

Preparation time: 20 minutes
Cooking time: 25 minutes
Ready-in time: 45 minutes
Serving size: 4 people

Ingredients:
1 large sweet potato, peeled and cut into 1/2-inch strips
2 cups sushi rice, cooked and seasoned
4 sheets nori (seaweed)
1 avocado, sliced
1 cucumber, julienned
2 tablespoons sesame seeds, toasted
1/4 cup soy sauce
1/4 cup pickled ginger
1 tablespoon wasabi paste
1 tablespoon olive oil
Salt, to taste

Instructions:

First, we begin with the star of the roll – the sweet potato. Preheat your oven to 400°F (200°C). Toss the sweet potato strips with olive oil and a pinch of salt. Spread them evenly on a baking sheet and roast for about 25 minutes, or until they are tender and slightly caramelized at the edges. The transformation of the humble sweet potato into a golden delight is pure magic.

While the sweet potatoes are roasting, prepare your sushi station. Lay out your bamboo mat and have a bowl of water handy to keep those fingers moist and the rice from sticking.

Place a sheet of nori on the bamboo mat, shiny side down. Wet your hands and gently spread a thin layer of sushi rice over the nori, leaving a 1-inch border at the top. This is where we infuse our intention into each grain – patience and care.

Sprinkle a light shower of toasted sesame seeds over the rice. Now, arrange the roasted sweet potato strips, avocado slices, and cucumber julienne in a horizontal line across the center of the rice.

With confidence, lift the edge of the bamboo mat closest to you and begin to roll it away, tucking the filling tightly as you go. Continue rolling until you reach the border. Moisten the edge of the nori with a bit of water and seal the roll.

Using a sharp knife, slice the roll into 8 even pieces, wiping the blade with a damp cloth between cuts for a clean, precise presentation. Repeat the process with the remaining ingredients.

Serve your Sweet Potato Rolls with soy sauce, pickled ginger, and a dab of wasabi. Each bite is a symphony of textures – the crisp cucumber, creamy avocado, and the velvety sweet potato – a true comfort in every layer.

And there you have it, the Sweet Potato Roll, offering a gentle embrace to your taste buds. Until next time, may your culinary adventures be as vibrant and fulfilling as this delightful creation!

59. Mushroom Medley Roll: Umami Richness

Mushrooms are like nature's little treasure chests, each one packed with unique flavors and textures. This roll brings together an orchestra of mushrooms to deliver a symphony of umami that will dance on your taste buds.

Preparation time: 20 minutes
Cooking time: 15 minutes
Ready-in time: 35 minutes
Serving size: 4 people

Ingredients:
1 cup sushi rice
1 1/4 cups water
1/4 cup rice vinegar
1 tablespoon sugar
1/2 teaspoon salt
2 tablespoons vegetable oil
1 cup shiitake mushrooms, thinly sliced
1 cup oyster mushrooms, thinly sliced
1 cup enoki mushrooms, trimmed
2 tablespoons soy sauce
1 tablespoon mirin
4 sheets nori
1 avocado, thinly sliced
1 small cucumber, julienned
Pickled ginger, for serving
Soy sauce, for dipping

Instructions:

First, let's prepare our foundation, the sushi rice. Rinse the sushi rice under cold water until the water runs clear. Combine the rice and water in a rice cooker and let it work its magic. Once done, transfer the rice to a large bowl and allow it to cool slightly. In a small bowl, mix the rice vinegar, sugar, and salt until dissolved, then gently fold this mixture into your rice.

Next, heat up a pan with vegetable oil over medium heat. Toss in the shiitake, oyster, and enoki mushrooms. Sauté these beauties for about 5 minutes until they soften and release their juices. Add soy sauce and mirin to the pan, letting the mushrooms absorb these flavors for another 3 minutes. Once done, let them cool slightly.

Now, let's roll! Place a sheet of nori on a bamboo sushi mat, shiny side down. Wet your hands to prevent sticking, then spread a thin layer of sushi rice over the nori, leaving a 1-inch border at the top. Arrange a mix of our sautéed mushrooms, avocado slices, and cucumber julienne in a line across the center of the rice.

Using the bamboo mat, roll the nori tightly over the fillings, pressing gently but firmly to seal. You can dampen the border with a bit of water to help it stick. Repeat the process with the remaining ingredients.

Finally, slice each roll into bite-sized pieces with a sharp knife, cleaning the blade with a damp cloth between cuts. Serve your mushroom medley rolls with pickled ginger and soy sauce on the side.

Ah, the humble mushroom has transformed into a star on your sushi stage! Enjoy this roll's umami symphony and let each bite transport you to a forest of flavors. Until next time, keep exploring and let your culinary journey be filled with joy!

60. Eggplant Nigiri: Grilled Perfection

Eggplant Nigiri is a symphony of flavors and textures. Imagine the smoky char of perfectly grilled eggplant, combined with the delicate sweetness of sushi rice, all harmonizing in one bite. Let's embark on this culinary journey together and create a masterpiece that's both humble and extraordinary.

Preparation time: 20 minutes
Cooking time: 10 minutes
Ready-in time: 30 minutes
Serving size: 4 people

Ingredients:
1 large eggplant
2 cups sushi rice, cooked and seasoned
2 tablespoons soy sauce
1 tablespoon mirin
1 tablespoon sake
1 teaspoon sugar
1 tablespoon sesame oil
1 teaspoon sesame seeds, toasted
4 nori sheets, cut into thin strips
Pickled ginger, for garnish
Wasabi, for serving
Fresh chives, finely chopped, for garnish

Instructions:

First, we begin with our star ingredient – the eggplant. Slice the eggplant into thin, even pieces, about a quarter-inch thick. You want each slice to be a perfect canvas for your nigiri. Now, in a small bowl, whisk together the soy sauce, mirin, sake, and sugar. Let the sugar dissolve and create a beautiful marinade.

Brush each eggplant slice generously with the marinade. Heat a grill pan over medium-high heat and add a touch of sesame oil. Once it's shimmering, lay the eggplant slices on the pan. Grill each side for about 2-3 minutes, until they're soft and have those gorgeous grill marks.

While the eggplant is grilling, let's focus on the sushi rice. Wet your hands to prevent sticking, and form the seasoned sushi rice into small, oval-shaped mounds. Each mound should fit perfectly in your palm, like a small treasure.

Now, gently lay a slice of grilled eggplant over each mound of rice. Use a strip of nori to wrap around the middle, securing the eggplant to the rice. This not only adds flavor but also that classic nigiri look.

For the final touch, sprinkle each piece with toasted sesame seeds and a few finely chopped chives. Serve your Eggplant Nigiri with pickled ginger and a touch of wasabi on the side. Each bite will be a delightful contrast of smoky, sweet, and savory flavors.

And there you have it, the Eggplant Nigiri: a humble vegetable transformed into a work of art. Keep grilling, keep exploring, and remember – every dish is a journey. Until next time, may your kitchen be filled with joy and your plates with perfection!

Advanced Sushi Techniques

61. Flamed Nigiri: A Touch of Fire

The dance of flames meeting fresh fish is an act of culinary poetry. This dish brings a theatrical flair to your table, as the gentle kiss of fire transforms delicate nigiri into something extraordinary. Let's ignite your sushi journey with a touch of fire!

Preparation time: 20 minutes
Cooking time: 5 minutes
Ready-in time: 25 minutes
Serving size: 4 people

Ingredients:
200g sushi-grade salmon, thinly sliced
200g sushi-grade tuna, thinly sliced
2 cups sushi rice, cooked and seasoned
4 tablespoons soy sauce
1 tablespoon wasabi
2 green onions, finely chopped
1 lemon, thinly sliced
Sushi ginger, for serving
Microgreens, for garnish
A small bowl of water (for handling the rice)
A culinary torch

Instructions:

First, let's prepare our sushi rice. You know the drill: rinse the rice until the water runs clear, then cook it to perfection. Once cooked, season it with a mixture of rice vinegar, sugar, and salt. Now, let it cool to room temperature.

Now, with our seasoned rice ready, it's time to shape it. Wet your hands with a little water to prevent sticking, and grab a small amount of rice. Shape it into an oblong mound with a gentle squeeze.

Next, drape a slice of sushi-grade salmon or tuna over each rice mound, pressing gently to adhere. You've got the basics down; now let's add the magic of fire.

Take your culinary torch and, with a steady hand, lightly sear the surface of the fish. You're looking for a slight char that brings out the rich, buttery flavors of the fish without cooking it through. This step is pure theater, so enjoy the process!

Once all your nigiri are kissed by the flame, arrange them beautifully on a platter. Garnish with a touch of wasabi, a sprinkle of finely chopped green onions, and a few microgreens for a pop of color. Add a lemon slice on the side for a zesty twist.

Serve your flamed nigiri with soy sauce and sushi ginger. Watch your guests' faces light up as they take their first bite, experiencing the perfect blend of textures and flavors.

"Bravo! You've just elevated your sushi game to a sizzling new level. Remember, the dance of fire and fish is all about balance – a little char, a lot of love. Until next time, keep your flame bright and your sushi spectacular!"

62. Ceviche Roll: Fusion Freshness

Sometimes, the ocean's bounty calls for a dance of flavors. Imagine the zest of ceviche meeting the elegance of sushi. This roll is a vibrant celebration of cultures, where every bite is a refreshing wave of fusion creativity. Ready your taste buds!

Preparation time: 30 minutes
Cooking time: 10 minutes
Ready-in time: 40 minutes
Serving size: 4 people

Ingredients:
1 cup sushi rice
1 ¼ cups water
2 tablespoons rice vinegar
1 tablespoon sugar
½ teaspoon salt
1 pound sashimi-grade white fish (e.g., halibut), diced
1 small red onion, finely chopped
1 jalapeño, seeded and minced
1 cup fresh cilantro, chopped
1 avocado, sliced
1 cucumber, julienned
1 tomato, diced
Juice of 4 limes
1 sheet nori (seaweed)
Soy sauce, for serving
Wasabi, for serving
Pickled ginger, for serving

Instructions:

First, let's get that sushi rice going. Rinse the rice under cold water until the water runs clear. Combine the rice and water in a rice cooker and let it do its magic. Once cooked, transfer the rice to a large bowl, and while it's still hot, mix in the rice vinegar, sugar, and salt. Stir gently to avoid smashing the grains, and let it cool to room temperature.

Now, let's prepare the ceviche. In a medium bowl, combine the diced white fish, red onion, jalapeño, cilantro, tomato, and lime juice. Give it a good mix and let it marinate in the refrigerator for about 10 minutes. The acidity from the lime juice will the fish, giving it a fresh and tangy flavor.

While the ceviche is marinating, lay out your bamboo sushi mat and place a sheet of plastic wrap over it. On top of the plastic wrap, lay down the nori sheet. Spread an even layer of sushi rice over the nori, pressing gently with your fingers.

Once the rice is set, arrange the marinated ceviche, avocado slices, and cucumber julienne in a line across the center of the rice. Carefully lift the edge of the mat and begin to roll, pressing gently but firmly to keep it tight. Continue rolling until you have a perfect sushi roll.

Using a sharp knife, slice the roll into bite-sized pieces. Serve your Ceviche Roll with soy sauce, wasabi, and pickled ginger on the side.

"Bravo! You've just created a symphony of flavors on your plate. This Ceviche Roll is not just a dish; it's an experience. Share it with friends, and let the fusion feast begin!"

cook

63. Oshizushi: Pressed Perfection

In the heart of Osaka, where the streets teem with life and the air is filled with the aroma of street food, lies a hidden gem of Japanese cuisine – Oshizushi. This pressed sushi, with its meticulous layers and precise flavors, is a symphony on your taste buds.

Preparation time: 1 hour
Cooking time: 30 minutes
Ready-in time: 1 hour 30 minutes
Serving size: 4 people

Ingredients:
2 cups sushi rice
2 ½ cups water
¼ cup rice vinegar
2 tablespoons sugar
1 teaspoon salt
200 grams fresh salmon, thinly sliced
200 grams fresh tuna, thinly sliced
1 small cucumber, julienned
½ avocado, thinly sliced
1 sheet nori, cut into strips
Soy sauce, for serving
Wasabi, for serving
Pickled ginger, for serving

Instructions:

Alright, let's dive into this culinary journey! Start by rinsing the sushi rice under cold water until the water runs clear. This removes excess starch. Cook the rice with the measured water in a rice cooker or on the stovetop. Once it's cooked, let it sit for about 10 minutes to steam.

In a small bowl, mix the rice vinegar, sugar, and salt until fully dissolved. Fold this mixture into the warm rice, ensuring every grain is coated with this sweet, tangy blend. Let the rice cool to room temperature.

Now, let's set up our oshizushi mold. If you don't have one, a small rectangular container lined with plastic wrap will do the trick. Begin by layering your thinly sliced salmon at the bottom of the mold. Next, add a layer of rice, pressing it down firmly but gently. Then, layer the tuna, followed by another layer of rice. Continue this process, alternating with cucumber, avocado, and nori strips, always pressing the rice firmly.

Once all layers are assembled, cover the mold with the lid or another piece of plastic wrap. Press down firmly to compact the layers together. Let it sit for about 10 minutes. Carefully remove the lid and flip the mold onto a cutting board. Slice the oshizushi into bite-sized pieces using a sharp, wet knife to prevent sticking.

Place your beautiful creations onto a serving platter. Serve with soy sauce, wasabi, and pickled ginger on the side. Each bite is a testament to the harmony of flavors and textures.

Bravo! You've just crafted a piece of Osaka's rich culinary heritage. Enjoy each bite as the layers unfold on your palate, much like a story waiting to be told. Remember, the art of sushi is a journey, not a destination. Until our next culinary adventure!

64. Uramaki Mastery: Inside-Out Roll

In the heart of sushi artistry, the inside-out roll, or uramaki, stands as a testament to the beauty of breaking traditions. Let's take a journey where rice becomes the canvas, and flavors dance in perfect harmony.

Preparation time: 30 minutes
Cooking time: 20 minutes
Ready-in time: 50 minutes
Serving size: 4 people

Ingredients:
2 cups sushi rice
2 1/2 cups water
1/2 cup rice vinegar
2 tablespoons sugar
1 teaspoon salt
4 sheets nori (seaweed)
200 grams sashimi-grade tuna or salmon, sliced into strips
1 avocado, sliced
1 cucumber, julienned
2 tablespoons sesame seeds, toasted
Soy sauce, for serving
Pickled ginger, for serving
Wasabi, for serving

Instructions:

First, let's get that sushi rice perfect. Rinse the sushi rice under cold water until the water runs clear. This washes away the excess starch. Combine the rice and water in a rice cooker and cook according to the rice cooker's instructions. Once cooked, let it sit for 10 minutes to steam.

While the rice is cooking, mix the rice vinegar, sugar, and salt in a small bowl until dissolved. Gently fold this mixture into the cooked rice, using a wooden spoon or spatula. Spread the rice out on a large baking sheet to cool to room temperature.

Lay a sheet of plastic wrap over a bamboo sushi mat. Place a nori sheet, shiny side down, on the plastic wrap. Wet your hands with water to prevent sticking, and spread a thin layer of sushi rice evenly over the nori, pressing gently.

Now, here's the magic trick: flip the nori and rice over, so the rice is on the bottom. Line the center with strips of sashimi-grade tuna or salmon, avocado slices, and julienned cucumber.

Using the bamboo mat, carefully roll the sushi into a tight cylinder. Sprinkle toasted sesame seeds over the rice. Press gently to ensure they stick.

With a sharp knife, slice the roll into 8 pieces, cleaning the knife with a damp cloth between cuts for clean edges. Serve your masterpiece with soy sauce, pickled ginger, and a dab of wasabi.

Congratulations, you've rolled your way into sushi greatness! Every slice tells a story of precision and passion. Now, share this creation with friends and let the flavors transport you to a serene sushi haven.

65. Chirashi Bowl: Scattered Sushi Beauty

In the bustling streets of Tokyo, there's a culinary masterpiece that captures the essence of sushi in a single bowl. This Chirashi Bowl is an explosion of colors, textures, and flavors that dance together in perfect harmony. Ready to embark on this delightful journey?

Preparation time: 25 minutes
Cooking time: 20 minutes
Ready-in time: 45 minutes
Serving size: 4 people

Ingredients:
2 cups sushi rice
2 1/2 cups water
1/4 cup rice vinegar
2 tablespoons sugar
1 teaspoon salt
1/2 pound sashimi-grade tuna, sliced
1/2 pound sashimi-grade salmon, sliced
1/4 pound cooked shrimp, halved
1 avocado, sliced
1 cucumber, julienned
2 sheets nori, cut into thin strips
1 tablespoon sesame seeds
2 tablespoons soy sauce
1 tablespoon mirin
1 tablespoon sake
1 teaspoon wasabi paste
4 shiso leaves, torn
Pickled ginger, for serving

Instructions:

First things first, we need to make the sushi rice. Rinse the rice under cold water until the water runs clear. Combine the rice and water in a rice cooker and let it cook. Once it's done, let it sit for about 10 minutes to steam.

While the rice is cooking, let's prepare the seasoning. In a small saucepan, combine rice vinegar, sugar, and salt. Heat this mixture over low heat until the sugar dissolves completely. When the rice is ready, transfer it to a large bowl and gently fold in the vinegar mixture. Remember, be gentle! We want fluffy, seasoned rice, not mashed rice.

Now, let's move on to our toppings. In a small bowl, mix soy sauce, mirin, sake, and wasabi paste. This will be our flavorful drizzle. Arrange the tuna, salmon, shrimp, avocado, and cucumber in a visually appealing manner atop the rice. Scatter the nori strips and sesame seeds over the top.

Drizzle the soy mixture evenly over the bowl, then add the shiso leaves. Serve your Chirashi Bowl with a side of pickled ginger to cleanse the palate between bites.

If you've ever wanted to experience the beauty of a sushi chef's artistry in a single dish, this Chirashi Bowl is your ticket. Dive in, savor every bite, and let the flavors transport you to Japan. Until next time, keep your knives sharp and your spirit sharper!

66. Temari Sushi: Ball-Shaped Elegance

Imagine the harmony of flavors delicately wrapped in a stunning spherical form, each bite offering a symphony of taste and texture. Temari Sushi is not only a feast for the palate but a visual delight that will impress your guests and elevate your sushi-making prowess.

Preparation time: 30 minutes
Cooking time: 20 minutes
Ready-in time: 50 minutes
Serving size: 4 people

Ingredients:
Sushi rice: 2 cups cooked and seasoned
Assorted sashimi-grade fish (tuna, salmon, yellowtail): 12 thin slices
Cooked shrimp: 4 large, halved lengthwise
Cucumber: 1, thinly sliced into rounds
Avocado: 1, thinly sliced
Radish: 4, thinly sliced
Soy sauce: for serving
Wasabi: for serving
Pickled ginger: for serving
Plastic wrap: as needed

Instructions:

Alright, let's get rolling... or should I say, let's get balling! Start with your perfectly cooked and seasoned sushi rice. If you haven't seasoned your rice yet, make sure to mix it with some rice vinegar, sugar, and salt while it's still warm. Trust me, this step is crucial for that authentic sushi flavor.

Now, set your workspace with all your beautiful ingredients prepared and ready to go. We're talking thin slices of sashimi-grade fish, cucumber, avocado, radish, and halved shrimp. The fresher, the better – your taste buds will thank you later.

Grab a piece of plastic wrap and lay it flat on your countertop. Place a slice of fish or a piece of shrimp in the center. Add a small amount of sushi rice on top of the fish, about the size of a small golf ball. Don't go crazy with the rice – we're aiming for elegance here.

Carefully gather the edges of the plastic wrap and twist them together, forming a tight ball. Give it a gentle squeeze to ensure everything holds together nicely. Then, unwrap your little masterpiece and voila, you've got your first Temari Sushi! Repeat this process with the rest of your ingredients, mixing and matching to create a vibrant assortment.

Once all your Temari Sushi balls are complete, arrange them on a beautiful platter. Serve them with soy sauce, wasabi, and pickled ginger on the side. Each bite should be a burst of flavor, a moment of sushi bliss.

Congratulations, sushi maestro! You've just added a touch of ball-shaped elegance to your culinary repertoire. Remember, the true essence of sushi lies in the balance of flavors and the artistry of presentation. Until next time, may your kitchen be filled with joy and creativity!

67. Gunkan Maki: Battleship Sushi

Ah, the Gunkan Maki! Imagine a tiny sushi boat, braving the vast ocean of flavors. This sushi is not just a dish; it's an adventure on your plate. Prepare to set sail!

Preparation time: 20 minutes
Cooking time: 15 minutes
Ready-in time: 35 minutes
Serving size: 4 people

Ingredients:
Sushi rice - 2 cups, cooked
Rice vinegar - 2 tbsp
Sugar - 1 tbsp
Salt - 1 tsp
Nori sheets - 2, cut into 2-inch wide strips
Tobiko (flying fish roe) - 1/2 cup
Ikura (salmon roe) - 1/2 cup
Scallions - 2, finely chopped
Wasabi - for serving
Soy sauce - for serving

Instructions:

Alright, let's embark on this culinary voyage! First, take your warm, freshly cooked sushi rice. To that, add your rice vinegar, sugar, and salt. Mix it gently but thoroughly, ensuring every grain is coated. We want that perfect balance of sweet, sour, and salty.

Now, grab your nori sheets. They're like the sails of our little sushi boats. Cut them into strips about 2 inches wide. We need them to be sturdy enough to hold our precious cargo.

Next, with damp hands (to prevent sticking), take a small ball of sushi rice, about the size of a walnut, and shape it into an oval. Wrap a strip of nori around the rice, leaving the top exposed. Press the nori gently to secure it, and voila! You've made the hull of your Gunkan Maki.

Now, it's time to load our boats. For the first batch, carefully spoon a generous portion of tobiko on top of the rice, filling the nori cylinder just to the brim. Do the same with the ikura for the second batch. The vibrant colors of the roe contrast beautifully against the white rice and dark nori.

Top each piece with a sprinkle of finely chopped scallions. This adds a refreshing crunch and a burst of flavor that's simply irresistible.

Serve your Gunkan Maki with a dollop of wasabi on the side and a small dish of soy sauce for dipping. Each bite is an explosion of textures and tastes—truly a journey worth every step.

"Congratulations, sushi sailors! You've crafted a fleet of Gunkan Maki that would make any sushi chef proud. Now, let these little battleships of flavor conquer your taste buds. Enjoy the voyage!"

68. Narezushi: Traditional Fermentation

In the heart of ancient Japan, fermentation was an art mastered by few. Narezushi, a time-honored delicacy, embodies the spirit of patience and tradition. Let's embark on this culinary journey, transforming humble fish and rice into a piece of history on your plate.

Preparation time: 30 minutes (excluding fermentation)
Cooking time: 20 minutes
Ready-in time: 6 months
Serving size: 4 people

Ingredients:
1 whole mackerel, cleaned and gutted
2 cups sushi rice
3 cups water
1 cup sea salt
6 cups cooked rice
2 tablespoons sake
4 tablespoons rice vinegar
Banana leaves or cheesecloth for wrapping

Instructions:

First, we start with our mackerel. After cleaning and gutting your fish, generously rub it inside and out with sea salt. This is going to draw out the moisture and begin the preservation process. Place the salted fish in a container, cover it, and let it rest in the refrigerator for about 10 days.

Once the mackerel has hardened and released its excess liquid, rinse it thoroughly to remove the salt. Now, pat it dry and prepare to wrap it in banana leaves or cheesecloth. This wrapping will allow the fish to breathe while it ferments.

Next, take your sushi rice and rinse it until the water runs clear. Cook the rice with the measured water in a rice cooker or on the stove. Once the rice is cooked, let it cool slightly before mixing in the sake and rice vinegar. Spread the rice out to cool completely.

Now, layer a bed of the cooked rice mixture in a fermentation container. Place the mackerel on top of the rice bed, then cover it completely with the remaining rice. Press down firmly to ensure there are no air pockets, as this can spoil the fermentation process.

Cover the container tightly and store it in a cool, dark place. The fermentation process will take about 6 months, during which the mackerel will transform into a tangy, savory delight. Check occasionally to ensure everything is proceeding well, but do not disturb it too much.

After 6 months, your narezushi is ready to be unveiled. Gently remove the fish from the rice, slice it thinly, and serve it with a fresh bowl of rice or on its own. The flavors are bold, complex, and a testament to the passage of time.

Congratulations, you've just created a masterpiece that bridges the past and present! Enjoy each bite of this ancient delicacy, knowing you've mastered a piece of culinary history. Until next time, keep exploring the depths of flavor and tradition!

69. Sushi Cake: Layered Celebration

Imagine a dish that brings the artistry of sushi to a new height, a celebration in every layer that dazzles both the eyes and the palate. This Sushi Cake is more than just food; it's a culinary masterpiece designed to be the star of any gathering.

Preparation time: 40 minutes
Cooking time: 20 minutes
Ready-in time: 60 minutes
Serving size: 4 people

Ingredients:
2 cups sushi rice
2 ½ cups water
¼ cup rice vinegar
2 tablespoons sugar
1 teaspoon salt
200 grams sashimi-grade tuna, thinly sliced
200 grams sashimi-grade salmon, thinly sliced
1 avocado, thinly sliced
1 cucumber, julienned
4 sheets nori (seaweed)
2 tablespoons sesame seeds
1 tablespoon wasabi, for serving
Soy sauce, for serving
Pickled ginger, for serving

Instructions:

First, let's get that sushi rice perfectly cooked. Rinse the rice under cold water until it runs clear. Combine the rice and water in a rice cooker. Once the rice is done, let it sit for 10 minutes to steam. Meanwhile, mix the rice vinegar, sugar, and salt until they dissolve. Fold this mixture gently into the cooked rice, and let it cool to room temperature.

Now, let's build our masterpiece. Line an 8-inch springform pan with plastic wrap, ensuring it hangs over the edges for easy removal. Place a sheet of nori at the bottom of the pan. Spread a third of the sushi rice evenly over the nori, pressing it down gently with damp fingers.

Arrange half of the tuna slices over the rice, followed by a layer of avocado slices and a sprinkle of sesame seeds. Add another sheet of nori and spread another third of the rice over it. This time, layer the salmon slices and cucumber, finishing with another sprinkle of sesame seeds.

Top it off with the final sheet of nori and the last layer of rice. Press everything down firmly but gently. Wrap the overhanging plastic wrap over the top and refrigerate for at least 30 minutes to set.

When you're ready to serve, carefully remove the Sushi Cake from the pan and unwrap the plastic. Use a sharp, damp knife to slice it into wedges, just like a cake. Serve with wasabi, soy sauce, and pickled ginger.

Creating this Sushi Cake is like painting a canvas with flavors and textures. It's a joy that brings people together, a shared celebration of culinary artistry. Remember, in every slice, there's a story waiting to be told. Enjoy every bite as if it's your first.

70. Kurozushi: Black Rice Innovation

Imagine a sushi roll that not only excites your taste buds but also dazzles your eyes with its vibrant hues. Let's embark on a journey where tradition meets avant-garde!

Preparation time: 30 minutes
Cooking time: 20 minutes
Ready-in time: 50 minutes
Serving size: 4 people

Ingredients:
2 cups black rice
2 1/4 cups water
1/4 cup rice vinegar
2 tablespoons sugar
1 teaspoon salt
8 sheets of nori
1 avocado, sliced
1 cucumber, julienned
200g fresh sashimi-grade tuna, sliced
4 tablespoons tobiko (flying fish roe)
Soy sauce, for serving
Pickled ginger, for serving
Wasabi, for serving

Instructions:

First, let's cook our black rice. Rinse the rice under cold water until the water runs clear. In a medium pot, combine the black rice and water. Bring it to a boil, then reduce the heat to low, cover, and let it simmer for about 20 minutes. Once cooked, fluff the rice with a fork and let it cool slightly.

While the rice is cooling, prepare the sushi seasoning. In a small saucepan, combine the rice vinegar, sugar, and salt. Heat over low heat, stirring until the sugar and salt dissolve. Remove from heat.

Transfer the slightly cooled rice to a large bowl. Gradually fold in the sushi seasoning with a wooden spoon or spatula, making sure to mix gently to avoid mashing the rice. Allow the seasoned rice to cool to room temperature.

Lay a sheet of nori, shiny side down, on a bamboo sushi mat. With damp hands, spread a thin layer of black rice over the nori, leaving a 1-inch border at the top. Arrange a few slices of avocado, cucumber, and tuna horizontally across the center of the rice.

Using the bamboo mat, carefully roll the sushi away from you, pressing gently but firmly to form a tight roll. Wet the border with a bit of water to seal the roll. Repeat with the remaining ingredients.

Slice each roll into 6-8 pieces with a sharp knife, wiping the blade with a damp cloth between cuts to ensure clean slices. Arrange the Kurozushi on a serving platter, garnishing with a sprinkle of tobiko for a burst of color.

Serve with soy sauce, pickled ginger, and a dab of wasabi on the side.

"Every bite of this Kurozushi is a dance of flavors and textures, a testament to the beauty of innovation in culinary tradition. Enjoy this vibrant creation, and let it inspire your own sushi-making adventures!"

71. Sweet Mochi Sushi: Chewy Delight

Imagine a world where sushi meets the delightful chewiness of mochi! This Sweet Mochi Sushi is an enchanting fusion that will surprise your taste buds and take you on a whimsical culinary journey. Let's craft this delightful treat together!

Preparation time: 30 minutes
Cooking time: 10 minutes
Ready-in time: 40 minutes
Serving size: 4 people

Ingredients:
1 cup glutinous rice flour (mochiko)
1/4 cup granulated sugar
1 cup water
1/2 cup sweetened red bean paste (anko)
1/4 cup potato starch (for dusting)
1 ripe mango, thinly sliced
1 kiwi, thinly sliced
1/4 cup desiccated coconut
1 tablespoon honey

Instructions:

Alright, let's get started! First, in a mixing bowl, combine the glutinous rice flour and sugar. Add the water gradually while stirring until everything is well blended and smooth. Now, pour this mixture into a microwave-safe dish. We're going to microwave it on high for about 2 minutes. Give it a good stir and then pop it back in for another minute or so until it becomes a sticky, elastic dough.

Next, dust your work surface generously with potato starch. Carefully transfer the hot mochi dough onto the surface. Dust your hands with the starch too—trust me, you'll thank me later. Now, gently knead the dough a few times until it's workable without sticking to everything.

Divide the mochi dough into 8 equal pieces. Flatten each piece into a small round disc. Place about a teaspoon of sweetened red bean paste in the center of each disc and fold the edges over to encase the filling, shaping them into small balls.

Now, let's get fruity! Take your thin slices of mango and kiwi and arrange them on top of each mochi ball, pressing gently so they stick. Drizzle a touch of honey over the fruit and sprinkle some desiccated coconut on top for that extra flair.

And there you have it—Sweet Mochi Sushi, a chewy and delightful twist on traditional sushi. Enjoy these with friends or savor them all to yourself!

Ah, the sweet symphony of mochi and fresh fruit, a playful dance on the palate! May this delightful creation bring joy and a touch of whimsy to your sushi repertoire. Until our next culinary adventure, happy cooking!

72. Fruit Sushi Roll: Nature's Candy

Ever wondered how sushi could be sweet and savory, all at once? Let's dive into the whimsical world of fruit sushi, where nature's candy takes center stage, blending tradition with a burst of fresh, fruity flavors.

Preparation time: 30 minutes
Cooking time: 10 minutes
Ready-in time: 40 minutes
Serving size: 4 people

Ingredients:
1 cup sushi rice
1 1/4 cups water
2 tablespoons rice vinegar
1 tablespoon sugar
1/2 teaspoon salt
1 mango, thinly sliced
1 kiwi, thinly sliced
10 strawberries, thinly sliced
1 banana, thinly sliced
1/2 cup shredded coconut
4 sheets of nori (seaweed)
Honey for drizzling
Mint leaves for garnish

Instructions:

First, let's prepare the sushi rice. Rinse the rice under cold water until the water runs clear. Combine the rice and water in a rice cooker, and let it cook. Once done, transfer the rice to a large bowl. While it's still warm, gently fold in the rice vinegar, sugar, and salt. This will give the rice that tang and stickiness.

Now, the fun part begins! Lay out a bamboo sushi mat and place a sheet of nori on top. With damp fingers, spread a thin layer of sushi rice over the nori, leaving about an inch at the top edge. Sprinkle a handful of shredded coconut over the rice to add a hint of tropical flair.

Arrange the fruit slices in a colorful line along the center of the rice. Imagine creating a rainbow with the mango, kiwi, strawberries, and banana. Carefully roll the sushi, using the mat to help shape it into a tight log. Repeat with the remaining ingredients.

Using a sharp knife, slice each roll into bite-sized pieces. It's crucial to clean the knife between cuts to ensure clean, beautiful slices.

For a finishing touch, drizzle a little honey over the top and garnish with fresh mint leaves. This not only enhances the presentation but also adds a touch of sweetness and aroma.

"Creating these fruit sushi rolls is like painting a canvas with nature's most vibrant colors. Enjoy this playful twist on traditional sushi, and let your taste buds dance with delight!"

73. Matcha Roll: Green Tea Sweetness

In the heart of Japan, matcha is more than just tea; it is an art, a ritual, and a flavor that dances on the palate. Today, we transform this treasured ingredient into a dessert roll that sings with green tea sweetness.

Preparation time: 20 minutes
Cooking time: 15 minutes
Ready-in time: 35 minutes
Serving size: 4 people

Ingredients:
4 large eggs
100g granulated sugar
90g all-purpose flour
10g matcha powder
1 tsp baking powder
2 tbsp milk
150ml heavy cream
2 tbsp powdered sugar
1 tsp vanilla extract
Extra matcha powder for dusting

Instructions:

Alright, let's embark on this delicious journey together. First, preheat your oven to 180°C (350°F) and line a baking sheet with parchment paper. Now, separate the egg whites from the yolks. In a mixing bowl, whisk the egg yolks with half of the granulated sugar until it turns pale and fluffy. This is where the magic begins!

In another bowl, sift together the flour, matcha powder, and baking powder. Gradually fold this dry mixture into the yolk mixture, adding the milk to create a smooth batter.

Next, beat the egg whites in a clean bowl until they form soft peaks. Slowly add the remaining sugar, beating until stiff peaks form. Gently fold the egg whites into the matcha batter, taking care not to deflate the mixture. Pour the batter onto the prepared baking sheet and spread it evenly.

Bake for about 12-15 minutes, or until the sponge is springy to the touch. While it's baking, whip the heavy cream with powdered sugar and vanilla extract until it holds firm peaks.

Once the sponge is ready, turn it out onto a clean tea towel dusted with powdered sugar and peel off the parchment paper. Roll the sponge up with the towel and let it cool. This step is crucial for creating that perfect roll shape.

After it's cooled, unroll the sponge and spread the whipped cream evenly over it. Roll it back up without the towel and place it seam-side down on a plate. Dust with extra matcha powder for that finishing touch.

And there you have it, a Matcha Roll that bridges the elegance of tea ceremonies with the joy of dessert! Enjoy every bite, and remember, the secret ingredient is always a touch of love and a dash of creativity.

74. Coconut Rice Delights: Tropical Treat

Imagine the first bite of something that transports you to a sun-drenched island, where the waves gently caress the shore, and the air is thick with the scent of tropical fruits. That's what these coconut rice delights promise – a perfectly balanced adventure for your palate.

Preparation time: 20 minutes
Cooking time: 25 minutes
Ready-in time: 45 minutes
Serving size: 4 people

Ingredients:
1 cup sushi rice
1 cup coconut milk
1 cup water
2 tablespoons sugar
1/2 teaspoon salt
1 ripe mango, sliced
1 kiwi, sliced
1/4 cup shredded coconut, toasted
2 tablespoons fresh mint, chopped

Instructions:

First, my friends, we start by giving our sushi rice a good rinse under cold water. This is a crucial step; we are washing away the excess starch, ensuring our rice cooks up nice and fluffy. Once rinsed, combine the rice, coconut milk, water, sugar, and salt in a medium saucepan. Bring this heavenly mixture to a gentle boil over medium heat.

As it starts to bubble, reduce the heat to low, cover the pot, and let it simmer for about 18-20 minutes. Remember, patience is key here. You'll know it's ready when the liquid has been absorbed, and the rice is tender. Turn off the heat and let it sit covered for an additional 5 minutes.

While our rice is resting, let's prepare the fruit. Slice the mango and kiwi into thin, beautiful pieces. Their vibrant colors will make our dish as pleasing to the eyes as it is to the taste buds.

Fluff the rice with a fork and let it cool slightly before assembling our tropical treat. On a serving plate, shape the coconut rice into small, delightful mounds – almost like little islands. Top each mound with slices of mango and kiwi, letting the fruits cascade down the sides.

To finish, sprinkle the toasted shredded coconut generously over the top and garnish with a touch of fresh, chopped mint. The aroma alone will have you dreaming of palm trees and ocean breezes.

"Ah, there you have it – a dish that brings the tropics to your table. Enjoy each bite and let your taste buds embark on a journey far away. Until next time, keep exploring, keep tasting, and keep the spirit of adventure alive in your kitchen!"

75. Chocolate Sushi: Decadent Indulgence

Imagine blending the artistry of sushi with the opulence of chocolate. This fusion is not just a dish but a symphony of flavors that will leave your taste buds dancing. Ready to embark on a sweet journey like no other?

Preparation time: 30 minutes
Cooking time: 10 minutes
Ready-in time: 40 minutes
Serving size: 4 people

Ingredients:
1 cup sushi rice
1 ¼ cups water
2 tablespoons sugar
2 tablespoons rice vinegar
1 tablespoon cocoa powder
1 teaspoon vanilla extract
8 ounces dark chocolate, melted
1 large banana, sliced into strips
½ cup fresh strawberries, sliced thinly
¼ cup desiccated coconut
¼ cup crushed almonds
Chocolate sauce, for drizzling

Instructions:

Let's start by preparing the sushi rice. Rinse the rice under cold water until the water runs clear. This is crucial to get rid of excess starch. Add the rice and water to a saucepan, bring it to a boil, then reduce the heat to low, cover, and let it simmer for about 15 minutes. Once done, let it sit covered for an additional 10 minutes.

While the rice is cooking, combine the sugar, rice vinegar, cocoa powder, and vanilla extract in a small bowl. Stir until the sugar and cocoa powder are completely dissolved.

Transfer the cooked rice to a large bowl and gently fold in the cocoa mixture. Be patient—this is where the magic starts. The rice absorbs the flavors, creating a subtle yet rich chocolate essence.

Now, let's get creative. Lay out your bamboo mat and cover it with plastic wrap. Spread a thin layer of the chocolate rice over the mat, leaving an inch at the top free. Arrange the banana and strawberry slices in the center of the rice.

Using the bamboo mat, roll the sushi away from you, pressing gently but firmly to create a tight roll. Wet the exposed edge with a bit of water to seal the roll. Repeat the process with the remaining rice and fillings.

Once your rolls are ready, it's time to coat them in melted dark chocolate. Using a brush or spoon, generously cover each roll with the melted chocolate. Sprinkle the desiccated coconut and crushed almonds on top for added texture and flavor. Allow the chocolate to set for a few minutes.

With a sharp knife, slice each roll into bite-sized pieces. Arrange them on a serving platter and drizzle with chocolate sauce for an extra touch of indulgence.

Ah, look at this masterpiece! Who knew sushi could be so sweet? This chocolate sushi is not just a dessert; it's a conversation starter. Enjoy this delightful creation and remember, in the world of sushi, the only limit is your imagination!

76. Berry Bliss Roll: A Juicy Explosion

In the dance of flavors, sometimes the most unexpected partners create the most exhilarating performances. This Berry Bliss Roll is a juicy, vibrant testament to the magic that happens when you let your culinary imagination run wild.

Preparation time: 20 minutes
Cooking time: 10 minutes
Ready-in time: 30 minutes
Serving size: 4 people

Ingredients:
1 cup sushi rice
1 1/4 cups water
1 tablespoon rice vinegar
1 tablespoon sugar
1/2 teaspoon salt
1 nori sheet
1/2 cup strawberries, thinly sliced
1/2 cup blueberries
1/2 cup raspberries
1/4 cup cream cheese, softened
Mint leaves for garnish

Instructions:

First, let's prepare our sushi rice. Rinse the sushi rice under cold water until the water runs clear. Combine the rice and water in a saucepan, bring to a boil, then reduce the heat to low and cover. Let it simmer for about 10 minutes or until all the water is absorbed. Remove from heat and let it sit covered for another 10 minutes.

While the rice is resting, mix the rice vinegar, sugar, and salt in a small bowl until dissolved. Once the rice is ready, gently fold in the vinegar mixture. Spread the rice out on a baking tray to cool to room temperature.

Now, let's construct our Berry Bliss Roll. Place a bamboo sushi mat on a clean, flat surface. Lay the nori sheet on the mat, shiny side down. With wet hands, evenly spread a thin layer of sushi rice over the nori, leaving a 1-inch border at the top.

Next, add a line of cream cheese across the center of the rice. Arrange the strawberry slices, blueberries, and raspberries on top of the cream cheese. For an extra touch of freshness, add a few mint leaves.

To roll, lift the edge of the bamboo mat closest to you, and begin rolling the nori over the filling. Use the mat to shape and tighten the roll as you go. Once rolled, give it a gentle squeeze to secure.

Slice the roll into bite-sized pieces using a sharp knife dipped in water. Arrange beautifully on a serving platter and garnish with a few extra mint leaves for that final flourish.

And there you have it, a Berry Bliss Roll that bursts with a symphony of flavors and textures. It's like a sweet serenade that dances on your palate. Until our next culinary adventure, keep experimenting and let your kitchen be your stage!

77. Mango Sticky Rice Sushi: Exotic Flavor

Imagine a perfect fusion where the tropical sweetness of ripe mango meets the comforting, creamy texture of sticky rice. This sushi is not only a treat for the taste buds but an adventure for the senses. Prepare to be transported to an exotic place with every bite!

Preparation time: 20 minutes
Cooking time: 30 minutes
Ready-in time: 50 minutes
Serving size: 4 people

Ingredients:
1 cup glutinous rice
1 1/2 cups water
1 cup coconut milk
1/4 cup sugar
1/2 teaspoon salt
2 ripe mangoes, peeled and thinly sliced
1 tablespoon sesame seeds, toasted
Nori sheets (optional, for sushi rolls)
Mint leaves for garnish (optional)

Instructions:

First, my friends, we begin with the soul of the dish—the glutinous rice. Rinse it thoroughly under cold water until it runs clear. This step is crucial for achieving that perfect sticky texture. Once rinsed, combine the rice and water in a rice cooker. Let it cook until the rice is tender and delightfully sticky.

While the rice cooks, let's turn our attention to the coconut sauce. In a small saucepan over medium heat, combine the coconut milk, sugar, and salt. Stir continuously until the sugar dissolves completely, but be careful not to let it boil. We want a smooth and silky sauce.

When the rice is ready, transfer it to a mixing bowl and gently fold in the coconut sauce. Allow it to sit for about 10 minutes, giving the rice time to soak up all that creamy goodness.

Now, it's time to assemble our exotic sushi. Lay out a bamboo mat covered with plastic wrap if you have one. If not, a clean surface will do. Place a small portion of sticky rice on your mat or surface, pressing it gently to form a rectangle.

Layer thin slices of ripe mango over the rice. If you like, you can place a strip of nori underneath before adding the mango for a more traditional sushi roll. Roll it up tightly, using the mat or your hands to shape it.

Once rolled, carefully slice the sushi into bite-sized pieces. Sprinkle toasted sesame seeds over the top for an extra crunch and a hint of nuttiness. Garnish with fresh mint leaves for a pop of color and added freshness.

And voila, your Mango Sticky Rice Sushi is ready to be savored. Enjoy each bite slowly, letting the flavors dance on your palate.

Ah, you've done it! A masterpiece in the kitchen, a delight on the table. Remember, cooking is not just about following a recipe—it's about expressing your soul on a plate. Until next time, keep exploring, keep tasting, and keep creating magic in your kitchen!

78. Cinnamon Apple Roll: Cozy Comfort

Imagine the warmth of cinnamon-infused apples wrapped in a delicate sushi roll, a perfect harmony of East meets West. This recipe captures the essence of comfort, transforming a classic into an unexpected delight.

Preparation time: 30 minutes
Cooking time: 15 minutes
Ready-in time: 45 minutes
Serving size: 4 people

Ingredients:
1 cup sushi rice, cooked and cooled
1 tablespoon sugar
1 teaspoon cinnamon
1 apple, thinly sliced
1 tablespoon butter
1 tablespoon brown sugar
1 tablespoon lemon juice
4 sheets of nori
Honey or maple syrup for drizzling
Powdered sugar for dusting

Instructions:

First, let's talk about the rice. You've got your sushi rice already cooked and cooled, right? Now, mix in the tablespoon of sugar and the teaspoon of cinnamon. This will infuse the rice with a hint of sweetness and spice, a perfect base for our roll.

Next, in a skillet over medium heat, melt your butter. Add the apple slices, brown sugar, and lemon juice. Sauté this delightful mixture until the apples are tender and caramelized, which should take about 5 to 7 minutes. Let them cool slightly.

Lay out your nori sheets on a bamboo mat, rough side up. Spread a thin layer of the cinnamon-sugar rice over the nori, leaving about an inch at the top free of rice. Make sure to press the rice down gently but firmly.

Arrange the caramelized apple slices in a line across the center of the rice. Now, here comes the fun part: rolling. Lift the edge of the bamboo mat closest to you, and start rolling the nori over the apple slices, pressing gently but firmly. Keep rolling until you reach the end of the nori sheet.

Once rolled, use a sharp knife to cut the roll into bite-sized pieces. Drizzle a bit of honey or maple syrup over each piece and dust lightly with powdered sugar. Your Cinnamon Apple Roll is now ready to dazzle and delight.

Ah, the joy of blending flavors and cultures! This Cinnamon Apple Roll is like a warm hug on a chilly day. Enjoy every bite, and remember, the best creations come from the heart. Until next time, keep rolling with passion and creativity!

79. Pineapple Pleasure Roll: Juicy Sweetness

In the heart of summer, when the air is thick with warmth and the sun gleams brightest, we find ourselves craving something vibrant and refreshing. This roll, bursting with the joy of pineapple, is a tribute to those sun-kissed days.

Preparation time: 30 minutes
Cooking time: 15 minutes
Ready-in time: 45 minutes
Serving size: 4 people

Ingredients:
1 cup sushi rice
1 1/4 cups water
2 tablespoons rice vinegar
1 tablespoon sugar
1/2 teaspoon salt
4 nori sheets
1/2 fresh pineapple, thinly sliced into strips
1 cucumber, julienned
1 avocado, thinly sliced
8 imitation crab sticks
1 tablespoon sesame seeds, toasted
Soy sauce, for serving
Pickled ginger, for serving
Wasabi, for serving

Instructions:

First, let's get that sushi rice perfect. Rinse the sushi rice under cold water until the water runs clear. Combine the rice and water in a rice cooker and let it work its magic. Once cooked, transfer the rice to a large bowl. Gently mix in the rice vinegar, sugar, and salt while it's still warm. Let it cool to room temperature.

Lay a bamboo sushi mat on a flat surface and cover it with plastic wrap. Place a nori sheet, shiny side down, on the mat. Wet your hands slightly to prevent sticking and grab a handful of cooled sushi rice. Spread it evenly over the nori, leaving a 1-inch border at the top.

Sprinkle a pinch of toasted sesame seeds over the rice. Now for the juicy centerpiece—arrange a few strips of pineapple, cucumber, avocado, and crab sticks horizontally across the middle of the rice.

Using the bamboo mat, carefully lift the edge nearest to you and start rolling it over the filling. Keep the roll tight by gently pressing the mat while rolling. When you reach the top border, moisten it with a little water to seal the roll.

With a sharp knife, slice the roll into 8 pieces, wiping the blade with a damp cloth between cuts. Repeat the process with the remaining ingredients.

Serve your Pineapple Pleasure Rolls with soy sauce, pickled ginger, and a dab of wasabi on the side. Each bite is a tantalizing dance of sweet and savory.

Ah, the Pineapple Pleasure Roll—like a sweet melody of summer on your tongue. Remember, sushi isn't just food; it's an experience. Enjoy each bite, and let the flavors take you on a journey. Until next time, happy rolling!

80. Sweet Bean Roll: Traditional Twist

Embracing the balance of tradition and innovation, this Sweet Bean Roll offers a harmonious blend of flavors that dance on the palate. A delightful twist on classic sushi, it encapsulates the essence of East meets West in every bite.

Preparation time: 30 minutes
Cooking time: 20 minutes
Ready-in time: 50 minutes
Serving size: 4 people

Ingredients:
1 cup sushi rice
1 1/4 cups water
2 tablespoons rice vinegar
1 tablespoon sugar
1/2 teaspoon salt
1/2 cup sweet red bean paste (anko)
4 sheets nori (seaweed)
1 ripe mango, thinly sliced
1 small cucumber, julienned
1 tablespoon black sesame seeds
Soy sauce, for serving

Instructions:

First, let's awaken the rice. Rinse your sushi rice under cold water until the water runs clear. This step is like a morning shower for the grains, washing away the excess starch. Once refreshed, combine the rice with water in a rice cooker and let it cook until tender and fluffy.

While the rice is cooking, let's get the vinegar mixture ready. In a small bowl, mix the rice vinegar, sugar, and salt until it dissolves completely. This sweet-sour concoction will be the soul of our sushi rice.

As the rice cooker beeps, signaling its completion, transfer the hot rice to a large bowl. Pour the vinegar mixture over it while gently folding the rice with a wooden paddle. This step is crucial – we are infusing each grain with flavor while cooling it to room temperature. Patience, my friend, patience.

Now, lay out the nori sheets on a bamboo mat, shiny side down. Moisten your hands with water to prevent sticking and spread a thin, even layer of the seasoned sushi rice over the nori, leaving a small border at the top edge. Sprinkle with black sesame seeds for an artistic touch.

Next, the heart of our roll – sweet red bean paste. Smooth a line of anko across the center of the rice. Lay the mango slices and cucumber strips alongside the anko, adding a refreshing crunch and a burst of color.

Time to roll! Using the bamboo mat, roll the sushi tightly from the bottom, applying gentle pressure to keep everything snug. Seal the roll by moistening the top border of the nori with a dab of water.

With a sharp knife, slice the roll into bite-sized pieces. Arrange them on a lovely platter, ready to be enjoyed with soy sauce on the side.

Creating sushi is like painting a masterpiece; each roll tells a story of flavor and texture. Enjoy the symphony of sweet and savory in every bite. Until next time, keep the spirit of creativity alive in your kitchen!

81. Truffle Tuna Tartar: Gourmet Fusion

In this captivating dance of flavors, the delicate essence of tuna meets the opulent touch of truffle. It's a symphony for the palate, where simplicity harmonizes with luxury. Ready to embark on this culinary journey?

Preparation time: 20 minutes
Cooking time: 0 minutes
Ready-in time: 20 minutes
Serving size: 4 people

Ingredients:
300g fresh sashimi-grade tuna, finely diced
1 tbsp truffle oil
1 tbsp soy sauce
1 tsp yuzu juice
1 tsp finely grated ginger
1 avocado, finely diced
1 small cucumber, finely diced
2 tbsp finely chopped chives
Salt and pepper to taste
Microgreens for garnish
Toasted sesame seeds for garnish
Wonton crisps or toasted baguette slices for serving

Instructions:

First, let's prepare our lovely tuna. Make sure it's finely diced to perfection. Place the tuna in a chilled bowl to keep it as fresh as the sea breeze. Now, drizzle in the truffle oil and soy sauce. Ah, that's the aroma we're looking for! Add a splash of yuzu juice and grate some fresh ginger into the mix. Stir gently and let these flavors meld together.

Next, let's bring some vibrancy to our tartar. Dice the avocado and cucumber into small, delicate pieces. Add them to the bowl with the tuna. Sprinkle in the chives, and don't forget to season with a pinch of salt and pepper. Mix everything gently; we want each bite to be a perfect balance of texture and flavor.

Now, let's plate this masterpiece. Use a ring mold if you have one; it adds a touch of elegance. Divide the mixture into four portions and press it gently into the ring molds on individual plates. Carefully lift the molds to reveal perfectly shaped tuna tartar.

For the final flourish, garnish with microgreens and a sprinkle of toasted sesame seeds. Serve with wonton crisps or toasted baguette slices on the side. Each bite is a journey, a fusion of earth and ocean.

Ah, a dish fit for the gods! Share this with friends, and let the flavors speak of artistry and passion. Until our next culinary adventure, keep your knives sharp and your hearts hungry for more!

82. Kimchi Roll: Spicy Korean Influence

Ever wondered what happens when Korean zest meets the delicate art of sushi rolling? This Kimchi Roll is a delightful dance of flavors, where fermented spiciness intertwines with the subtlety of vinegared rice, creating an unforgettable culinary harmony.

Preparation time: 20 minutes
Cooking time: 20 minutes
Ready-in time: 40 minutes
Serving size: 4 people

Ingredients:
2 cups sushi rice, cooked and seasoned with rice vinegar
4 sheets of nori (seaweed)
1 cup kimchi, chopped
1 cucumber, julienned
1 carrot, julienned
1 avocado, sliced
4 oz. cooked shrimp, chopped
2 tablespoons sesame seeds
Soy sauce for dipping
Wasabi and pickled ginger for serving

Instructions:

Alright, let's get our sushi game on! First, make sure your sushi rice is perfectly cooked and seasoned. You know the drill – a bit of rice vinegar, sugar, and salt mixed in. Now, lay a bamboo mat on a flat surface and place a sheet of nori on it, shiny side down.

With slightly damp fingers, spread a thin layer of sushi rice over the nori, leaving about an inch at the top edge. Sprinkle a few sesame seeds over the rice for that extra nutty bite.

Time to introduce the stars! Arrange a line of chopped kimchi across the center of the rice. Next, add a few julienned cucumber and carrot sticks, some creamy avocado slices, and a generous sprinkle of chopped shrimp. It's all about balance here, my friends.

Now, wet the top edge of the nori with a bit of water. Using the bamboo mat, carefully roll the sushi away from you, pressing gently but firmly to keep everything together. Once you reach the end, give it a final press to seal.

With a sharp knife, slice the roll into bite-sized pieces. Clean the knife between cuts for those perfect, clean slices. Repeat with the remaining ingredients until you have a tempting array of Kimchi Rolls.

Serve your masterpiece with soy sauce, a dab of wasabi, and some pickled ginger. Each bite is a journey through flavors – spicy, tangy, fresh, and utterly satisfying.

Bravo, sushi artist! You've just created a fusion marvel that bridges cultures and tantalizes taste buds. Enjoy every bite, and remember, the world is your kitchen, and every dish is an adventure.

83. Wagyu Beef Roll: Luxurious Bite

Imagine the most sumptuous bite of sushi that melts like butter in your mouth. This Wagyu Beef Roll is the epitome of luxury, a true celebration for your taste buds. Each bite tells a story of elegance, flavor, and mastery.

Preparation time: 25 minutes
Cooking time: 5 minutes
Ready-in time: 30 minutes
Serving size: 4 people

Ingredients:
200 grams Wagyu beef, thinly sliced
2 cups sushi rice, cooked and seasoned
4 sheets nori (seaweed)
1 avocado, thinly sliced
1 cucumber, julienned
2 tablespoons soy sauce
1 tablespoon mirin
1 teaspoon wasabi
Pickled ginger, for serving
Soy sauce, for serving

Instructions:

Start by laying out your bamboo sushi mat and placing a sheet of plastic wrap over it. Put a sheet of nori on top of the plastic wrap, making sure the shiny side faces down. Spread half a cup of seasoned sushi rice evenly over the nori, leaving about an inch at the top.

Gently flip the nori so the rice is now facing down. Lay thin slices of Wagyu beef horizontally across the middle of the nori. Add a few slices of avocado and some julienned cucumber on top of the beef.

Now, it's time to roll! Using the bamboo mat, carefully roll the nori and rice over the fillings, pressing gently but firmly to ensure it holds together. Continue rolling until you reach the end of the nori. Wet the exposed edge of the nori with a little water to seal the roll.

Repeat with the remaining ingredients to make a total of four rolls. Using a sharp knife, slice each roll into six to eight pieces.

In a small bowl, mix the soy sauce and mirin for a dipping sauce. Serve your luxurious Wagyu Beef Rolls with a side of pickled ginger, a dab of wasabi, and the homemade dipping sauce.

Ah, the Wagyu Beef Roll—a true delight that combines the best of land and sea. Your guests will be talking about this luxurious bite for days. Enjoy every moment, every texture, every flavor. Until next time, may your kitchen be ever vibrant and your sushi rolls ever perfect!

84. Smoked Salmon Delight: A Smoky Twist

In the heart of culinary creation, there exists a harmony between tradition and innovation. Today, we embark on a flavorful journey where the delicate essence of smoked salmon dances with the spirit of sushi.

Preparation time: 20 minutes
Cooking time: 10 minutes
Ready-in time: 30 minutes
Serving size: 4 people

Ingredients:
1 cup sushi rice
1 1/4 cups water
2 tablespoons rice vinegar
1 tablespoon sugar
1/2 teaspoon salt
8 ounces smoked salmon, thinly sliced
1 avocado, thinly sliced
1 cucumber, julienned
4 sheets nori (seaweed)
1 tablespoon wasabi paste
1/4 cup soy sauce
Pickled ginger, for serving

Instructions:

Alright, let's get our hands into this culinary symphony. Start by rinsing the sushi rice under cold water until the water runs clear. Trust me, this step is vital for that perfect sticky texture. Toss the rice into a pot with the water, bring it to a boil, then lower the heat and let it simmer for about 10 minutes. Once it's done, let it rest off the heat for another 10 minutes.

While the rice is taking its nap, mix the rice vinegar, sugar, and salt until they dissolve. When the rice is ready and still warm, gently fold this mixture into the rice. Think of it as a delicate dance, not a wrestling match.

Now, place a sheet of nori on your bamboo mat, shiny side down. Moisten your hands to prevent the rice from sticking, and spread a thin layer of rice over the nori, leaving about an inch at the top edge.

Lay a few slices of smoked salmon down the center of the rice, followed by avocado and cucumber. Here's where the magic happens: roll the sushi away from you, using the mat to keep it tight. A little squeeze, but not too much; we want elegance, not a rice explosion.

Seal the roll by moistening the top edge of the nori with a bit of water. Slice your roll with a sharp knife, wetting the blade between cuts to ensure clean slices. Repeat this process with the remaining ingredients.

Serve your Smoked Salmon Delight with a dab of wasabi, soy sauce for dipping, and a side of pickled ginger. Each bite should be a smoky, creamy, and slightly tangy revelation.

Bravo! You've just crafted a masterpiece worthy of applause. Remember, each roll tells a story, and yours just sang a beautiful song. Until our next culinary adventure, keep your knives sharp and your flavors even sharper!

85. Sriracha Infusion Roll: Heat and Flavor

Imagine a symphony of flavors dancing on your palate, each note harmonized with a tantalizing kick of heat. That's exactly what you get with the Sriracha Infusion Roll – a masterpiece that celebrates the fusion of tradition and innovation.

Preparation time: 30 minutes
Cooking time: 10 minutes
Ready-in time: 40 minutes
Serving size: 4 people

Ingredients:
2 cups sushi rice, cooked and seasoned
4 sheets nori
1 avocado, thinly sliced
1 cucumber, julienned
1 carrot, julienned
200g fresh sashimi-grade tuna, thinly sliced
2 tablespoons Sriracha sauce
1 tablespoon mayonnaise
1 teaspoon soy sauce
1 teaspoon rice vinegar
1 teaspoon sesame seeds, toasted
Pickled ginger for serving
Soy sauce for dipping

Instructions:

Alright, let's embark on this flavorful journey. First, you'll want to make sure your sushi rice is perfectly cooked and seasoned. While the rice is cooling, mix the Sriracha sauce with mayonnaise and a touch of soy sauce and rice vinegar to create our spicy, creamy infusion.

Lay a sheet of nori on a bamboo sushi mat, shiny side down. Wet your hands to prevent the rice from sticking, and spread a thin layer of sushi rice evenly over the nori, leaving a small border at the top.

Next up, arrange the thinly sliced avocado, cucumber, and carrot in a horizontal line across the center of the rice. Place the fresh tuna slices on top of the vegetables. Now, drizzle a little of our Sriracha-mayo mixture over the tuna. This is where the magic happens!

Carefully lift the edge of the bamboo mat closest to you, and start rolling it away from you, pressing gently but firmly to keep everything tight. When you reach the border, wet it with a little water to seal the roll.

Use a sharp knife to cut the roll into bite-sized pieces. Sprinkle toasted sesame seeds over each piece for an added layer of texture and flavor. Arrange them on a beautiful platter, and serve with pickled ginger and soy sauce on the side.

And there you have it – a roll that's as vibrant as it is flavorful. Let each bite remind you that sushi is not just food; it's an experience, a story told through taste and texture. Enjoy the journey!

86. Caviar Crown Nigiri: A Royal Touch

Imagine the delicate balance of the ocean's finest treasures gracing your palate in a single bite. This nigiri, crowned with luxurious caviar, brings a regal elegance to your sushi experience.

Preparation time: 20 minutes
Cooking time: 10 minutes
Ready-in time: 30 minutes
Serving size: 4 people

Ingredients:
2 cups sushi rice
2 1/4 cups water
1/4 cup rice vinegar
2 tablespoons sugar
1 teaspoon salt
8 slices fresh tuna
8 slices fresh salmon
4 tablespoons premium caviar
Soy sauce, for serving
Wasabi, for serving
Pickled ginger, for serving

Instructions:

First, let's prepare the sushi rice. Rinse the rice under cold water until the water runs clear. This step is crucial for removing excess starch and achieving that perfect sushi texture. Add the rinsed rice and water to a rice cooker, and let it do its magic.

While the rice is cooking, let's prepare the rice seasoning. In a small saucepan over low heat, combine the rice vinegar, sugar, and salt. Stir until the sugar and salt have completely dissolved. Once done, set it aside to cool.

When the rice is ready, transfer it to a large bowl and gently fold in the vinegar mixture. Be careful not to smash the grains – you want each grain to remain distinct. Allow the seasoned rice to cool to room temperature.

Now, let's move on to the fish. Ensure your tuna and salmon are fresh and thinly sliced. This is where precision and a sharp knife come into play. Lay the slices out on a plate for easy assembly.

With damp hands, shape the sushi rice into small, bite-sized ovals. This is the foundation of your nigiri, so take your time to make them uniform and neat. Gently place a slice of tuna or salmon on each rice oval, pressing lightly to adhere.

And now, the crowning glory – the caviar. Using a small spoon, place a delicate dollop of caviar on top of each piece of nigiri. This is where the elegance shines, adding a touch of luxury to each bite.

Serve your Caviar Crown Nigiri with soy sauce, wasabi, and pickled ginger on the side.

With each piece, you'll feel like royalty savoring the finest sushi in the kingdom. May your culinary journey continue to be filled with flavors that dance and delight! Until next time, keep experimenting and enjoying the art of sushi.

87. Pesto Salmon Roll: Italian Inspiration

Ah, the fusion of cultures! Imagine the vibrant green fields of Italy meeting the serene waters of Japan. This Pesto Salmon Roll brings that dream to life, blending aromatic pesto with fresh salmon in a sushi roll that promises an explosion of flavors.

Preparation time: 20 minutes
Cooking time: 15 minutes
Ready-in time: 35 minutes
Serving size: 4 people

Ingredients:
2 cups sushi rice, cooked
4 sheets of nori (seaweed)
8 oz fresh salmon, thinly sliced
1/2 cup fresh basil pesto
1 avocado, thinly sliced
1/2 cucumber, julienned
1 tbsp rice vinegar
Salt, to taste
1 tbsp olive oil
Soy sauce, for serving
Pickled ginger, for serving
Wasabi, for serving

Instructions:

Alright, let's embark on this culinary journey! First, take your warm, cooked sushi rice and gently mix in the rice vinegar and a pinch of salt. This will give it that subtle zing we love in sushi rice. Now, spread out your bamboo sushi mat and place a sheet of nori on top, shiny side down.

Wet your hands to prevent the rice from sticking, and spread a thin, even layer of sushi rice over the nori, leaving about an inch free at the top edge. Now, here comes the twist! Spread a generous spoonful of fresh basil pesto across the center of the rice. This green goodness will infuse the roll with Italian flair.

Next, lay down those thin slices of fresh salmon, followed by the creamy avocado slices and the crisp cucumber julienne. The combination of textures, my friends, is what makes this roll truly magical.

It's time to roll! Carefully lift the bamboo mat and roll it away from you, pressing gently to keep the ingredients snug inside. Use a bit of water on the edge of the nori to seal the roll. Repeat the process with the remaining nori sheets and ingredients.

Once your rolls are complete, take a sharp knife and slice each roll into bite-sized pieces. Arrange them beautifully on a serving platter, and don't forget the soy sauce, pickled ginger, and a dab of wasabi on the side.

And there you have it, a Pesto Salmon Roll that's as much a feast for the eyes as it is for the palate.

Bravo, chef! You've just created a masterpiece that bridges continents and culinary traditions. Enjoy this delightful fusion and let each bite transport you to a world where Italian passion meets Japanese precision. Until next time, keep rolling with creativity and flavor!

88. Pickled Plum Roll: Umeboshi Tartness

Every bite of this roll is a journey through the heart of Japanese flavors, where the tartness of umeboshi dances with the crispness of fresh cucumber. It's a delightful symphony that will transport you straight to the vibrant streets of Tokyo.

Preparation time: 30 minutes
Cooking time: 20 minutes
Ready-in time: 50 minutes
Serving size: 4 people

Ingredients:
2 cups sushi rice
2 1/4 cups water
1/4 cup rice vinegar
2 tablespoons sugar
1 teaspoon salt
4 sheets nori (seaweed)
6 pickled plums (umeboshi), pitted and finely chopped
1/2 cucumber, julienned
1 avocado, thinly sliced
2 tablespoons sesame seeds, toasted
Soy sauce, for serving
Pickled ginger, for serving

Instructions:

Alright, let's get started with our Pickled Plum Roll. First things first, rinse the sushi rice under cold water until the water runs clear. This removes excess starch and gives us that perfect, sticky texture. Place the rice and water in a rice cooker and cook until it's done. If you're using a pot, bring the water and rice to a boil, then reduce the heat to low, cover, and cook for about 20 minutes. Let it rest for 10 minutes.

While the rice is cooking, mix the rice vinegar, sugar, and salt in a small saucepan over low heat until dissolved. Once your rice is ready and slightly cooled, fold the vinegar mixture into the rice. Be gentle—think of it as whispering to the grains, not smashing them.

Now, let's roll! Place a sheet of nori on a bamboo sushi mat, shiny side down. Wet your hands to prevent sticking and spread a thin layer of rice over the nori, leaving about an inch at the top edge. Sprinkle sesame seeds evenly over the rice.

In the center of the rice, lay a line of finely chopped umeboshi, followed by julienned cucumber and slices of creamy avocado. Using the mat, roll the nori tightly over the filling, applying gentle pressure to form a compact roll. Seal the edge with a bit of water.

Repeat with the remaining ingredients until you have four beautiful rolls. With a sharp knife, slice each roll into eight pieces, wiping the blade with a damp cloth between cuts to keep things clean.

Serve your Pickled Plum Roll with soy sauce and pickled ginger on the side. Enjoy the tartness and freshness with every bite!

Bravo! You've just mastered a roll that's both simple and profound. Every slice tells a story of balance and harmony. Share this creation with friends, and watch their faces light up with delight. Until next time, keep rolling and exploring new flavors!

89. Thai Basil Roll: A Fragrant Fusion

When you think of sushi, your mind might drift to the pristine shores of Japan. But today, let's embark on a journey to the bustling streets of Thailand, where fragrant basil and chili ignite your senses and merge with the delicate artistry of sushi.

Preparation time: 30 minutes
Cooking time: 10 minutes
Ready-in time: 40 minutes
Serving size: 4 people

Ingredients:
2 cups sushi rice
2 1/2 cups water
1/4 cup rice vinegar
2 tablespoons sugar
1 teaspoon salt
8 sheets nori
1/2 pound fresh tuna, thinly sliced
1 medium cucumber, julienned
1 medium carrot, julienned
1/4 cup fresh Thai basil leaves
1 avocado, sliced
2 tablespoons soy sauce
1 tablespoon fish sauce
1 Thai chili, finely chopped
1 lime, juiced
1 tablespoon sesame seeds, toasted

Instructions:

First, let's get that sushi rice just right. Rinse the rice under cold water until it runs clear. Combine the rice and water in a rice cooker and let it do its magic. Meanwhile, in a small saucepan, gently heat the rice vinegar, sugar, and salt until dissolved. Once the rice is cooked, fold in the vinegar mixture, but be kind to the grains – they've worked hard for you.

Lay out your bamboo sushi mat and place a sheet of nori on top, shiny side down. Moisten your fingers in a bowl of water and spread a thin layer of sushi rice over the nori, leaving a one-inch border at the top.

Arrange a few slices of tuna, cucumber, carrot, and avocado across the center of the rice. Now, here's the twist – sprinkle on some Thai basil leaves. They'll add a burst of fragrance and a splash of color.

Time to roll! Lift the edge of the mat closest to you and start rolling tightly, tucking in the filling as you go. Moisten the top border with a bit of water to seal the roll. Repeat with the remaining ingredients.

For the dipping sauce, mix the soy sauce, fish sauce, finely chopped Thai chili, and fresh lime juice in a small bowl. This sauce will add a zesty kick to each bite.

Slice your rolls into six to eight pieces, sprinkle with toasted sesame seeds, and serve with the dipping sauce on the side. Each bite is a melody of flavors – the fresh tuna, the crunch of vegetables, and the aromatic Thai basil harmonizing beautifully.

Ah, what a journey of flavors! I hope this Thai Basil Roll has brought a touch of the exotic to your sushi repertoire. Remember, the kitchen is your playground – don't be afraid to infuse your sushi with a bit of wanderlust. Until next time, happy rolling!

90. Jalapeño Tuna Roll: Spicy Zing

Imagine a burst of spice greeting the delicate flavors of fresh tuna, all encased in a perfect sushi roll. This adventurous creation brings together the heat of jalapeños with the cool, oceanic essence of tuna, creating a symphony of flavors that dance on your palate.

Preparation time: 20 minutes
Cooking time: 10 minutes
Ready-in time: 30 minutes
Serving size: 4 people

Ingredients:
2 cups sushi rice, cooked and seasoned
4 sheets nori (seaweed)
8 ounces fresh tuna, thinly sliced
2 jalapeños, thinly sliced
1 avocado, sliced
1 cucumber, julienned
Soy sauce, for dipping
Wasabi, for serving
Pickled ginger, for serving

Instructions:

First, gather all your ingredients and have them ready, because sushi making is all about precision and timing. Place a bamboo sushi mat on a flat surface and cover it with plastic wrap to prevent sticking. Lay a sheet of nori, shiny side down, on the mat.

Wet your hands with a little water to prevent the rice from sticking. Spread about half a cup of sushi rice evenly over the nori, leaving a 1-inch border at the top. Now, here's where the magic begins – place a few slices of fresh tuna, a couple of jalapeño slices, some avocado, and cucumber along the middle of the rice.

Using the bamboo mat, carefully roll the sushi away from you, applying gentle pressure to keep everything tight. When you reach the border, wet it slightly to seal the roll. Repeat this process with the remaining ingredients to make more rolls.

Once you have your rolls, use a sharp, wet knife to slice each roll into 8 pieces. Wipe the knife with a damp cloth between cuts to keep it clean and sharp. Arrange your beautifully crafted sushi on a platter.

Serve with soy sauce, a dab of wasabi, and pickled ginger. The combination of spicy jalapeño and tender tuna will surely captivate your senses and leave you craving more.

Ah, the joy of creating something so extraordinary from simple ingredients! Your kitchen is now a sushi haven, where flavors converge and the spirit of adventure thrives. Enjoy every bite, and remember, the art of sushi is as much about the journey as it is about the destination.

91. New Year's Osechi Roll: Celebration on Rice

The New Year is a time of renewal and celebration, and what better way to honor it than with a vibrant, elegant sushi roll? This Osechi Roll gathers traditional Japanese New Year's flavors into a single, festive bite.

Preparation time: 45 minutes
Cooking time: 20 minutes
Ready-in time: 1 hour 5 minutes
Serving size: 4 people

Ingredients:
2 cups sushi rice
2 1/4 cups water
1/4 cup rice vinegar
2 tablespoons sugar
1 teaspoon salt
4 sheets nori (seaweed)
4 slices of tamago (Japanese sweet omelet)
8 pieces of kamaboko (fish cake), sliced
1 small cucumber, julienned
8 cooked shrimp, deveined and halved
2 tablespoons ikura (salmon roe)
1 tablespoon black sesame seeds
Pickled ginger and wasabi for serving

Instructions:

Alright, let's get started! First, cook your sushi rice. Rinse it under cold water until the water runs clear. In a rice cooker, combine the rice and water, and let it cook. Once done, transfer the rice to a large bowl and let it cool slightly.

While the rice is still warm, mix the rice vinegar, sugar, and salt until they dissolve completely. Gently fold this mixture into the rice using a wooden spatula. You want to be gentle to avoid mashing the rice – think of it as a tender embrace.

Now, let's get rolling – literally! Place a sheet of nori on a bamboo sushi mat, shiny side down. Wet your hands and spread a thin layer of sushi rice over the nori, leaving about an inch at the top edge.

Layer the tamago slices, kamaboko, cucumber, and shrimp horizontally across the center of the rice. Now, lift the bamboo mat and start rolling away from you, pressing gently but firmly to keep the roll tight.

When you reach the edge, use a bit of water to seal the roll. Repeat this process with the remaining ingredients to make four beautiful rolls.

Cut each roll into eight pieces using a sharp, wet knife for a clean cut. Arrange the pieces on a platter, sprinkle with ikura and black sesame seeds for a pop of color and flavor.

Serve your New Year's Osechi Rolls with pickled ginger and a dab of wasabi on the side. This is a celebration on rice, after all!

"May your New Year be filled with joy and delectable bites! Remember, every roll tells a story, and this one is about starting fresh and savoring tradition. Happy rolling and even happier feasting!"

92. Spring Blossom Nigiri: Floral Essence

When cherry blossoms bloom, nature whispers secrets of renewal and beauty. This nigiri captures that ephemeral magic in every bite, an ode to the fleeting grace of spring.

Preparation time: 20 minutes
Cooking time: 15 minutes
Ready-in time: 35 minutes
Serving size: 4 people

Ingredients:
Sushi rice - 2 cups cooked and seasoned
Fresh salmon - 200 grams, thinly sliced
Edible cherry blossoms - 8, soaked in water for 10 minutes
Wasabi - to taste
Soy sauce - for serving
Pickled ginger - for garnish

Instructions:

Alright, let's get started! First, you want to prepare the sushi rice. Make sure it's cooked and seasoned to perfection. It should be sticky but not mushy – think of it as the canvas for our floral masterpiece.

Next, slice your fresh salmon into thin, delicate pieces. You want them to almost melt in your mouth – that's the level of finesse we're aiming for here. Lay them out on a clean cutting board, ready to be transformed.

Now, take your soaked edible cherry blossoms and gently pat them dry. These blossoms will add that unique touch of spring, both in flavor and aesthetics.

With your hands slightly damp to prevent sticking, shape the sushi rice into small, oblong mounds. Each one should fit comfortably in the palm of your hand – about the size of a small egg.

Place a small dab of wasabi on each rice mound. Not too much, unless you enjoy a fiery surprise!

Carefully drape a slice of salmon over each rice mound, pressing gently so it adheres. The fish should hug the rice snugly, like a silk kimono wrapping around a dancer.

Finally, place a cherry blossom on top of each piece of salmon. It's like adding the final stroke to a painting – absolutely essential.

Arrange your Spring Blossom Nigiri on a beautiful platter. Serve with soy sauce and pickled ginger on the side, and let the flavors of spring dance on your tongue.

Ah, you've done it! This nigiri is like poetry on a plate, a celebration of nature's fleeting beauty. Enjoy this culinary springtime serenade, and may every bite bring you closer to the essence of the season.

93. Summer Harvest Roll: Fresh Bounty

When the summer sun kisses the earth, the bounty of nature is at its peak. This roll captures the essence of the season, bringing together vibrant flavors and fresh ingredients. Let's dive into this culinary celebration of summer!

Preparation time: 30 minutes
Cooking time: 15 minutes
Ready-in time: 45 minutes
Serving size: 4 people

Ingredients:
Sushi rice, cooked and seasoned - 2 cups
Nori sheets - 4
Cucumber, julienned - 1
Carrot, julienned - 1
Mango, thinly sliced - 1
Avocado, thinly sliced - 1
Microgreens - 1/2 cup
Rice paper - 4 sheets
Soy sauce - for dipping
Pickled ginger - for serving
Wasabi - for serving

Instructions:

Alright, let's get rolling! First, make sure your sushi rice is perfectly cooked and seasoned with a mixture of rice vinegar, sugar, and salt. Spread a thin layer of this seasoned rice over a nori sheet, leaving about an inch at the top edge free for sealing.

Next, lay your julienned cucumber, carrot, and slices of mango and avocado in a neat, colorful row across the center of the rice. Sprinkle some microgreens for that extra burst of freshness.

Now, here's the fun part - rolling! Starting from the bottom edge, gently lift the nori sheet and roll it over the filling, pressing tightly as you go. Use a little water on the free edge to seal your roll. Repeat this process for the remaining nori sheets.

But wait, there's more! To give our roll a delightful summer twist, we're going to wrap each sushi roll in a sheet of softened rice paper. Dampen each rice paper sheet in warm water until it's pliable, then carefully wrap it around the sushi roll, giving it a beautiful, translucent finish.

Slice each roll into bite-sized pieces with a sharp, wet knife to ensure clean cuts. Arrange them on a platter, and serve with soy sauce, pickled ginger, and a dollop of wasabi on the side.

Crafting sushi is an art form, a dance of flavors and textures. Each bite is a journey through the season. Enjoy the vibrant notes of summer, and let every roll tell its own delicious story.

94. Autumn Squash Roll: Earthy Warmth

Autumn whispers through the golden leaves, inviting us to remember the warmth of harvest. In this roll, we embrace the soul of the season with the vibrant, earthy allure of squash, creating a symphony of flavors that dance on your palate.

Preparation time: 30 minutes
Cooking time: 20 minutes
Ready-in time: 50 minutes
Serving size: 4 people

Ingredients:
1 cup sushi rice
1 1/4 cups water
1/4 cup rice vinegar
1 tablespoon sugar
1 teaspoon salt
1 small butternut squash, peeled and thinly sliced
1 tablespoon olive oil
2 tablespoons soy sauce
1 avocado, thinly sliced
4 sheets nori (seaweed)
1 tablespoon toasted sesame seeds
Pickled ginger, for serving
Wasabi, for serving
Soy sauce, for serving

Instructions:

First, let's give our sushi rice the love it deserves. Rinse the rice in cold water until the water runs clear. Combine the rice and water in a rice cooker and let it work its magic. Once cooked, transfer the rice to a large bowl and let it cool slightly.

While the rice is cooking, preheat your oven to 400°F (200°C). Toss the butternut squash slices with olive oil and a pinch of salt, then arrange them on a baking sheet. Roast for about 20 minutes, or until tender and caramelized at the edges. Once done, let them cool to room temperature.

Next, let's season our sushi rice. In a small saucepan, gently heat the rice vinegar, sugar, and salt until dissolved. Pour this mixture over the cooked rice and fold it in with a slicing motion, ensuring each grain is delicately coated.

Now for the assembly! Place a sheet of nori on a bamboo sushi mat, shiny side down. With wet fingers, spread an even layer of seasoned sushi rice over the nori, leaving a 1-inch border at the top. Sprinkle with toasted sesame seeds for that extra crunch.

Lay a few slices of roasted butternut squash and avocado in a horizontal line across the center of the rice. Add a drizzle of soy sauce to elevate the flavors. Using the bamboo mat, roll the sushi tightly, applying gentle pressure to keep everything in place. Seal the roll by moistening the exposed edge of the nori with a bit of water.

Repeat the process with the remaining ingredients. Once all rolls are assembled, slice each roll into 8 pieces with a sharp knife, wiping the blade with a damp cloth between cuts.

Serve these autumnal delights with pickled ginger, wasabi, and soy sauce on the side.

Ah, the harmony of flavors in this roll sings of the season! As you savor each bite, may it transport you to a cozy autumn day where the air is crisp, and the harvest is bountiful. Enjoy this journey through nature's bounty!

95. Winter Wonderland Roll: Seasonal Comfort

Snowflakes drifting, a cozy fire crackling, and a sushi roll that captures the magic of winter. Let us embark on a culinary journey that brings warmth and joy to your table, even on the coldest of nights.

Preparation time: 30 minutes
Cooking time: 20 minutes
Ready-in time: 50 minutes
Serving size: 4 people

Ingredients:
2 cups sushi rice
2 1/4 cups water
1/4 cup rice vinegar
2 tablespoons sugar
1 teaspoon salt
4 nori sheets
8 ounces fresh salmon, thinly sliced
1 avocado, thinly sliced
1/2 cucumber, julienned
1/4 cup cream cheese, softened
1 tablespoon white sesame seeds, toasted
1 tablespoon black sesame seeds, toasted
1 tablespoon pickled ginger, finely chopped
Soy sauce, for dipping
Wasabi, for serving

Instructions:

First, let's get our sushi rice ready. Rinse the rice under cold water until the water runs clear. Then combine the rice and water in a rice cooker and let it work its magic. Once done, transfer the rice to a large bowl. While it's still warm, mix in the rice vinegar, sugar, and salt. Gently fold to combine and let it cool to room temperature.

Now, take your nori sheets and lay one shiny side down on a bamboo sushi mat. Wet your hands to prevent sticking and spread a thin layer of rice over the nori, leaving about an inch at the top edge. Sprinkle an even mix of white and black sesame seeds over the rice for an extra touch of flavor and texture.

Flip the nori over so the rice side is down on the mat. Arrange slices of fresh salmon, avocado, cucumber, and a thin line of softened cream cheese along the center of the nori. Add a sprinkle of finely chopped pickled ginger to give it a subtle zing.

Using the bamboo mat, carefully roll the sushi away from you, applying even pressure to keep it tight. When you reach the end, give it a gentle squeeze to seal the roll. Transfer to a cutting board and use a sharp knife to slice the roll into bite-sized pieces, wiping the knife with a damp cloth between cuts for clean slices.

Arrange your Winter Wonderland Rolls on a platter, and serve with soy sauce and a dab of wasabi on the side for the perfect finishing touch.

Well, there you have it! A sushi roll that delivers a warm embrace on a frosty evening. May your Winter Wonderland Rolls bring a smile to your face and a sparkle to your gatherings. Until next time, keep rolling with the seasons and savor every bite!

96. Cherry Blossom Festival Roll: A Festive Delight

Ah, the Cherry Blossom Festival! It's a time when nature's beauty blossoms in full glory. The delicate pink petals inspire a sushi roll that's as vibrant and festive as the spring festival itself. Let's bring the essence of cherry blossoms to your table with this delightful roll.

Preparation time: 30 minutes
Cooking time: 20 minutes (including rice cooking)
Ready-in time: 50 minutes
Serving size: 4 people

Ingredients:
2 cups sushi rice
2 1/2 cups water
1/4 cup rice vinegar
2 tablespoons sugar
1 teaspoon salt
4 sheets nori (seaweed)
8 ounces fresh tuna, thinly sliced
1 small cucumber, julienned
1 avocado, thinly sliced
2 tablespoons tobiko (flying fish roe)
1 tablespoon pickled ginger, finely chopped
1/4 cup sakura denbu (pink fish flakes)
Soy sauce, for serving
Wasabi, for serving
Pickled ginger, for serving

Instructions:

First, prepare the sushi rice. Rinse the rice under cold water until the water runs clear. Combine the rice and water in a rice cooker and cook according to the manufacturer's instructions. Once cooked, transfer the rice to a large bowl.

While the rice is still hot, mix the rice vinegar, sugar, and salt in a small bowl until dissolved. Pour this mixture over the rice and gently fold it in with a rice paddle, taking care not to mash the grains. Allow the rice to cool to room temperature.

Now, let's assemble the roll. Place a sheet of nori on a bamboo sushi mat, shiny side down. Wet your hands with water to prevent sticking and spread an even layer of rice over the nori, leaving a 1-inch border at the top edge.

Sprinkle a light layer of sakura denbu over the rice for that festive pink hue. Arrange the tuna slices, cucumber, avocado, and pickled ginger in a line across the center of the rice.

Using the bamboo mat, carefully roll the sushi away from you, tucking the ingredients in tightly as you go. Press the mat gently to shape the roll and seal the edge with a bit of water if needed.

Repeat with the remaining nori sheets and ingredients. Once all the rolls are assembled, slice each roll into 8 pieces with a sharp knife, wiping the blade with a damp cloth between cuts to ensure clean slices.

Arrange your Cherry Blossom Festival Rolls on a platter, sprinkle with tobiko, and serve with soy sauce, wasabi, and pickled ginger.

Itadakimasu! Enjoy the bursts of flavor and the playful colors on your plate. May this roll bring the joy of the Cherry Blossom Festival to your home. Until next time, keep your sushi dreams delicious and delightful!

97. Holiday Sparkle Nigiri: Festive Elegance

Imagine a snowy evening, twinkling lights, and the burst of flavors on your palate. This Holiday Sparkle Nigiri brings that festive magic to your sushi plate, blending tradition with a touch of holiday glamour.

Preparation time: 30 minutes
Cooking time: 15 minutes
Ready-in time: 45 minutes
Serving size: 4 people

Ingredients:
Sushi rice: 2 cups
Rice vinegar: 1/4 cup
Sugar: 2 tablespoons
Salt: 1 teaspoon
Fresh salmon: 8 ounces, thinly sliced
Fresh tuna: 8 ounces, thinly sliced
Fresh yellowtail: 8 ounces, thinly sliced
Avocado: 1, thinly sliced
Edible gold leaf: for garnishing
Microgreens: for garnishing
Wasabi: for serving
Soy sauce: for serving

Instructions:

Alright, my friends, let's start by preparing the sushi rice. Rinse the rice under cold water until the water runs clear. Cook it according to your rice cooker's instructions or the package directions. Once it's cooked, transfer it to a large bowl and let it cool slightly.

Now, in a small saucepan, combine the rice vinegar, sugar, and salt. Heat it gently until the sugar dissolves. Pour this mixture over the warm rice and gently fold it in with a spatula. Be careful not to smash the rice grains; we want them to stay fluffy.

Next, let's move on to the fish. Slice your salmon, tuna, and yellowtail into thin, even pieces. Each slice should be about the size of two fingers. If you're feeling adventurous, try slicing at an angle for a more elegant presentation.

With your rice cooled and seasoned, wet your hands with a mixture of water and vinegar to prevent sticking. Shape small, bite-sized mounds of rice, about the size of a large marble. Each mound should be firm but not too compact.

Lay a slice of fish over each rice mound, pressing gently to adhere. Now, for that festive touch, place a thin slice of avocado on top of some of the nigiri and add a tiny piece of edible gold leaf. This is where the sparkle comes in!

Arrange your Holiday Sparkle Nigiri on a beautiful platter. Garnish with microgreens for a pop of color. Serve with wasabi and soy sauce on the side, and watch as your guests' faces light up with delight.

May your holiday season be as bright and flavorful as this glittering creation! Remember, the joy of cooking lies not just in the taste but in the shared moments around the table. Happy sushi making, and may your festivities be filled with sparkle and joy!

98. Harvest Moon Roll: A Lunar Celebration

When the moon glows its fullest, there's magic in the air, and what better way to capture this enchantment than with a roll that reflects the bounty of the harvest and the ethereal beauty of the night sky?

Preparation time: 30 minutes
Cooking time: 20 minutes
Ready-in time: 50 minutes
Serving size: 4 people

Ingredients:
2 cups sushi rice, cooked and seasoned
4 sheets nori (seaweed)
1 small sweet potato, thinly sliced and tempura-fried
1 avocado, thinly sliced
4 ounces fresh tuna, thinly sliced
2 tablespoons black sesame seeds
1 small cucumber, julienned
2 tablespoons pickled radish, julienned
2 tablespoons unagi (eel) sauce
Soy sauce, for serving
Wasabi, for serving
Pickled ginger, for serving

Instructions:

Alright, let's embark on this culinary journey together! First, make sure your sushi rice is cooked and seasoned to perfection. This is your foundation—treat it with the respect it deserves. Now, take your nori sheets and lay one shiny side down on a bamboo sushi mat. Wet your hands slightly to prevent sticking and spread a thin, even layer of rice over the nori, leaving about an inch at the top edge clear.

Sprinkle the black sesame seeds generously over the rice. Flip the nori over gently so the rice side is down; this will be our outer layer, mimicking the night sky.

In the center of the nori, lay a few slices of tempura-fried sweet potato, followed by the avocado slices. These ingredients bring the warmth and richness of the harvest to our roll. Next, add a few slices of fresh tuna. The tuna symbolizes the moon's luminous glow—fresh and striking.

Take the julienned cucumber and pickled radish and lay them parallel to the other ingredients. These will add a crunchy texture and a burst of tangy flavor, making the roll exciting with each bite.

Now, for the fun part—rolling! Carefully use the bamboo mat to roll the nori and rice over the fillings, ensuring you keep it tight yet gentle. Wet the top edge of the nori to seal the roll completely. Use a sharp knife to cut the roll into even pieces—wipe the blade with a damp cloth between cuts to keep it clean.

Arrange your Harvest Moon Roll on a beautiful platter, drizzle unagi sauce generously over the top, and serve with soy sauce, wasabi, and pickled ginger on the side.

Ah, there it is! A masterpiece worthy of a lunar celebration. Remember, every bite you take is a tribute to the beauty of nature and the joy of culinary artistry. Enjoy this Harvest Moon Roll under the moonlight, and let your spirit soar among the stars!

99. Winter Citrus Roll: Bright and Refreshing

When winter's chill nips at our noses, we can find warmth and vitality in the brightness of citrus. This roll is a celebration of those zesty gems, bringing a burst of sunshine to your sushi experience.

Preparation time: 30 minutes
Cooking time: 20 minutes
Ready-in time: 50 minutes
Serving size: 4 people

Ingredients:
2 cups sushi rice, cooked
2 tablespoons rice vinegar
1 tablespoon sugar
1 teaspoon salt
4 sheets nori (seaweed)
1 orange, peeled and thinly sliced
1 grapefruit, peeled and thinly sliced
1 avocado, thinly sliced
1 small cucumber, julienned
4 ounces crab meat (real or imitation)
2 tablespoons orange zest
Soy sauce, for serving
Pickled ginger, for serving
Wasabi, for serving

Instructions:

Alright, let's get started. First, we need to prepare the sushi rice. After cooking your sushi rice, gently fold in the rice vinegar, sugar, and salt while it's still warm. This will give it that tang. Let the rice cool to room temperature.

Next, lay out your bamboo mat and place a sheet of nori on top, shiny side down. Wet your hands to prevent the rice from sticking, and spread a thin layer of sushi rice over the nori, leaving a small border at the top edge.

Arrange a few slices of orange, grapefruit, avocado, and cucumber horizontally across the rice. Add a bit of crab meat on top. Now, the zest comes into play – sprinkle some fresh orange zest over the filling to add that extra citrus punch.

Carefully lift the edge of the bamboo mat closest to you and start rolling it away from you. Keep it tight but gentle, as you don't want to squish the filling. Once you reach the end, give it a gentle squeeze to secure the roll.

Using a sharp knife, slice the roll into 6-8 pieces. It's helpful to wet the knife in between slices to get clean cuts. Repeat the process with the remaining ingredients to make all your rolls.

Serve your Winter Citrus Rolls with soy sauce, pickled ginger, and a touch of wasabi. The refreshing citrus flavors will dance on your tongue, making you forget all about winter's chill.

Just like that, a bit of winter sunshine on your plate! Remember, great sushi is about balance and harmony. Enjoy these bright bites, and may they bring warmth to your heart and soul. Until next time, keep rolling with joy!

100. Spring Pea Blossom Roll: A Verdant Welcome

The arrival of spring brings a burst of color and freshness to our plates. Imagine the delicate sweetness of spring peas, the crispness of fresh vegetables, and the elegance of blossom petals, all rolled into one. Let's create a symphony of flavors that welcomes the new season!

Preparation time: 30 minutes
Cooking time: 10 minutes
Ready-in time: 40 minutes
Serving size: 4 people

Ingredients:
1 cup sushi rice
1 1/4 cups water
2 tablespoons rice vinegar
1 tablespoon sugar
1/2 teaspoon salt
4 nori sheets
1 cup blanched spring peas
1/2 cup thinly sliced cucumber
1/2 cup julienned carrots
8 edible blossom petals (such as nasturtium or pansy)
1 ripe avocado, thinly sliced
Soy sauce, for serving
Pickled ginger, for serving
Wasabi, for serving

Instructions:

First, let's start with our sushi rice. Rinse the rice under cold water until the water runs clear. Place the rice and water in a rice cooker and cook according to the manufacturer's instructions. Once the rice is cooked, let it sit for 10 minutes to steam.

While the rice is steaming, combine the rice vinegar, sugar, and salt in a small saucepan over low heat. Stir until the sugar dissolves. Remove from heat and let it cool slightly.

Transfer the cooked rice to a large bowl and gently fold in the vinegar mixture. Be careful not to mash the rice. Allow it to cool to room temperature.

Now, let's prepare our fillings. Blanch the spring peas in boiling water for just a minute and then plunge them into ice water to retain their vibrant color. Pat them dry. Arrange all your ingredients—peas, cucumber, carrots, avocado, and blossom petals—within easy reach.

Place a nori sheet shiny side down on a bamboo sushi mat. Wet your hands to prevent sticking and spread a thin layer of sushi rice over the nori, leaving a 1-inch border at the top.

Arrange a line of spring peas, cucumber, carrots, avocado, and a few blossom petals across the center of the rice. Carefully lift the edge of the mat closest to you and start rolling away from you, applying gentle pressure to keep the roll tight. Seal the roll by moistening the top border with a bit of water.

Using a sharp knife, slice the roll into 8 even pieces. Repeat with the remaining nori sheets and fillings.
Serve your Spring Pea Blossom Rolls with soy sauce, pickled ginger, and a touch of wasabi. Each bite should be a celebration of springtime flavors!

Ah, the artistry of sushi never ceases to amaze! Every roll tells a story, and this one whispers the secrets of spring. Enjoy your culinary creation—it's as vibrant as the season itself. Until next time, keep rolling and keep smiling!

Thank you note and review request:

Thank you for cooking with

Sushi Mastery:

100 Recipes from Nakamoto's Kitchen

-

I hope you found the recipes as tasteful and delicious as I do.

If you did, then please show your support and love by leaving a review where you found the book.

Make sure to check out the rest of my books.

-

Happy Cooking,

Takeshi Nakamoto